Klaus Bockmuehl

The Challenge of Marxism

A Christian Response

InterVarsity Press
Downers Grove
Illinois 60515

Acknowledgment is made to the following for permission to reprint copyrighted material:

Scripture quotations, unless otherwise indicated, are from the Revised Standard Version of the Bible, copyrighted 1946, 1952, © 1971, 1973.

Quotations from Marx-Engels: Collected Works, I (1975), III (1975), IV (1975) and V (1976), are reprinted by permission of International Publishers.

The quote on pp. 163-64 is from Karl Jaspers, The Future of Mankind. © 1961 by the University of Chicago. Used by permission of the University of Chicago Press.

The lines by Goethe quoted in note #11, Chap. 3 are from Faust, part two, trans. Philip Wayne. © The Estate of Philip Wayne, 1959. Reprinted by permission of Penguin Books Ltd.

InterVarsity Press is the book-publishing division of Inter-Varsity Christian Fellowship, a student movement active on campus at hundreds of universities, colleges and schools of nursing. For information about local and regional activities, write IVCF, 233 Langdon St., Madison, WI 53703.

Distributed in Canada through InterVarsity Press, 1875 Leslie St., Unit 10, Don Mills, Ontario M3B 2M5, Canada.

First published under the title Herausforderungen des Marxismus © 1979 by Brunnen Verlag, Giessen and Basel.

ISBN 0-87784-816-5
Library of Congress Catalog Card Number: 79-9701

Printed in the United States of America

16   15   14   13   12   11   10   9   8   7   6   5   4   3   2
93   92   91   90   89   88   87   86   85   84   83   82   81   80

Part I

The Marxist Advance

Chapter 1

The New Appeal of Marxism

Today Marxism is the dominant ideology for many people, whether they like it or not. This is true not only for countries under Communist rule, but also for Western and Third-World countries, although admittedly in different ways.

One might, of course, seriously question whether Marxism is still alive in the hearts and minds of people in the Communist world. In 1976 a letter from the Swedish ambassador to Peking to his government in Stockholm inadvertently became public. He described the Soviet Union as an "empty volcano." The Soviet experiment, he said, had lost its appeal for people in the Communist world as well as for Western intellectuals.[1]

This fits the picture given recently in an anecdote in the British periodical *Encounter*. A visitor from the West called on a family in Moscow. The grandfather, a professor now more than ninety years old, had known Lenin personally. While the old gentleman was dressing for the occasion, his children and grandchildren confided to the visitor, "He is a nice fellow who likes to talk. But you should know one thing. He is still a Marxist. Please don't answer back too much to him. ..." This conversation, *Encounter* editors commented, could not have taken place in Moscow in 1910 or even in 1950.[2] It did in 1974.

Still a Viable Option?
The ideology of Marxism, however, has at least remained an important tool in the hands of Soviet leaders. Marxists understand that since the French Revolution we have lived in an age of ideology Because of the participation of the masses in political decision making (at least in theory), all government actions must be interpreted morally and ideologically in ordeı to be justified before the public. Western governments tend to think only in terms of national interest or economics rather than ideology. Therefore, government decisions are easier to attack because they appear selfish; they are not accompanied by a justification showing they are in the best interest of humanity. For the Soviets, then, Marxism remains an important instrument, even if only for foreign politics.

In the West today Marxism is the most potent alternative to the old way of life. This is true not only for the emerging leaders of Third-World nations, but also for the youth, particularly the university students of many industrialized and developing nations.

After World War 2 and the experience with National Socialism, many people were quick to conclude that mankind had reached "the end of the age of ideologies." But they forgot that men and women will always look for answers to questions of meaning: What is the purpose of history? What is the meaning of life for an individual? In the past Christianity supplied the answers to these questions, but now the ongoing process of secularization has created a spiritual vacuum which Marxism has entered and filled. In the non-Communist world today Marxism appears as the great giver of meaning to life—a fresh, unspent "real humanism" that most consistently applies the secular principles of atheism and the dominion of man over heaven and earth.

As a provider of meaning to life and as a savior from the spreading nihilism in the West, Marxism has been praised by many outstanding writers and accepted by not a small number of intellectually oriented youth who have grown up as atheists. "Eighty percent of the active students here are Marxists," a Christian fellowship secretary wrote me recently from one of the largest universities of Western Europe. We hear similar news from Latin America.

A middle class that has lost faith has nothing to pass on to its youth except a few material goods that would be available to them anyway. It has nothing to give in the way of deeper values and purposes. Its children are going astray spiritually.

It is possible that "the revolution dismisses its children," as Wolfgang Leonhard states in his autobiography, *Child of the Revolution*. But if so it certainly adopts the children of other people. The colossal tragedy evident in our intellectual and spiritual history caused one thoughtful observer to exclaim: "When it is possible that an ideology which produces walls, barbed-wire borders, minefields, and armies of refugees, is—in spite of all this—spreading as a surrogate of religion, how gigantic must the existing spiritual vacuum be!"[3] And even those who have been bitterly disappointed by the practice of Communism cling to it as the last straw, because nothing else seems to come close to saving them from nihilism.

In a somewhat different fashion Marxism in the West today has become a potent temptation for gifted, forward-looking young Christians, evangelicals among them. They are fascinated not so much by its radical secular humanism as by its socialism. Because evangelicals have little knowledge of Marxism, they identify Marxism with social reform and regard it as an energetic attempt to realize liberty, equality and fraternity or simply claim that Marxists are "for the poor." But even those Christians who try to avoid ignorance or naiveté regarding Marxism very often, under the pressure of mounting social problems, feel attracted to it because social ethics done from a genuinely Christian perspective is so hard to find.

Therefore, to those who feel they can no longer escape the challenge of today's "social questions" on a world scale, Marxism often seems to be the only adequate diagnosis and therapy. Even a complete turn from evangelicalism to Communism is possible, as can be seen in the life of one of the founding fathers of Marxism, Frederick Engels, who came from a strongly evangelical home. Such complete reversal can happen again today.

It is this effective new appeal of Marxism in the West which makes it necessary for Christians to begin to meet its ideological challenge. We need to know Marxism because it is the most vital doctrine of salvation in the secularized West, and we must be able to reply to it. In like manner, if we were living in India, we would need to be able to reply to Hinduism. If we are to be effective witnesses, we must be familiar with the salvation doctrines and alternative faiths that are offered in the marketplace.

Dealing with the challenge of Marxism is a long neglected part of the teaching task of the church. It is important for the entire Christian community, especially its younger generation. It is also needed to equip us for dialogue with the many people today who are partially influenced by a Marxist-tinted secularism. We need to understand their thinking, and to be able to converse with them we need to learn the terminology and concepts.

Christians must be able to formulate their message so it can be understood by Marxists of conviction and inclination, by those who stand between Marxism and Christianity, and by those who have left the Christian church for Marxism, some of them because their Christian parents were blind to social problems.

In studying these questions, moreover, we aim to strengthen our own faith in a turbulent time. Christians are a race taught to be patient. Politically and ideologically they often are the "quiet in the land" (Ps. 35:20). But today we are living at an hour in which even the dregs of wine are being drunk. This can be seen in such things as the thrust and influence of pornography and the propaganda for abortion.

In the field of theology, too, developments in recent years have gone to such an extreme that one can no longer remain silent. Theological debates no longer deal with details of the doctrines of creation or eschatology, or even with the more basic questions of Christology and the authority of Scripture, but with the fundamental question: atheism or not, God's kingdom or the kingdom of man. The whole ideological battle of our times has been reduced to this basic level. Christians today are being asked to spell out their faith and give sufficient reasons for it.

Encountering Marxism without external political pressures, as we may do in the West, can also have the salutary effect of producing self-criticism, the discovery of one's own defects. Meeting Marxism induces Christians to confront Christian truth with everyday reality. The confrontation of Christianity and Marxism is meant especially to serve us in this way. Surely Christians must seek and will find all their standards of self-assessment in the New Testament. But there is hardly a segment of Christendom which does not have certain peculiar traditions which persistently conceal part of the biblical doctrine and instruction. Thus, the challenge of Marxism to Christians not only functions as a mirror, but also as a forceful vacuum cleaner which will remove all manner of dust from behavior and doctrine. *Any* ideological confrontation necessitates deciding what we will stand for under all circumstances and what we may, or even must, abandon.

What Is Marxism?

Before we go further we must be clear about the range of meaning of the term *Marxism*. Here it is important to listen to what today's Marxists and Marx's original documents say. Marxism is more than a battle for social equality.[4] Marxism is also more than a program for agricultural reform, for instance, the dividing up of large properties among the former farm laborers. We know that moves of this kind in countries where Communists rose to power have been only transitory, ultimately giving way to large state-owned or cooperative kolkhoz units. Marxism is not just a specific economic system by which the means of production are nationalized with the aim of a strictly centralized, planned economy.

Marxism is furthermore not just socialism or communism. Learning to distinguish these terms is an absolutely basic requirement of dealing with social theory today. *Socialism* (from the Latin word *socialis*, best translated as "cooperative") and *communism* (from the Latin word *communis*, denoting "joint" or "collective") both mean much the same thing. They both denote the program to establish a social or collective instead of individual arrangement for certain needs and manifestations of human life. Such arrangements we call the socialization of certain areas of production or consumption (think of producer or consumer cooperatives).

But further distinctions need to be made. The extent of socialization may vary widely. Such socialization can take place either in free, voluntary cooperatives or in compulsory state socialism. And it can apply to certain sectors or to the whole of production and consumption. Even in so-called capitalist or free-enterprise countries in the West, there are a large number of industries which have been communalized or nationalized. Many countries have collectivized their transit systems, either on the level of the community (like local bus companies) or the state. Furthermore, the mail, garbage disposal, water supplies and a number of other branches of production and service, including education and hospitals are largely or entirely socialized. In the Communist bloc, on the other hand, certain small areas of economic life remain privately owned or are quietly being reprivatized as it seems to suit the economy.

Almost everywhere you can look back to a time in history when few goods and services were produced co-operatively. But here and there it has been thought useful or even necessary to do certain things collectively rather than leave them to the initiative and responsibility of individuals. And, on the other hand, we know of instances where nationalized or collectivized facilities have been returned to private ownership in order to increase efficiency or for other reasons. This has happened to a number of industries in Western countries, for instance in Britain and West Germany, as well as on a small scale in Eastern Europe, including craft shops and other small firms.

That different forms of socialism-communism can have widely differing goals, can be seen from a comparison between the original *Communist Manifesto* (1848) of Karl Marx and Frederick Engels and today's Socialist and Communist Party programs. In 1848, Marx and Engels seem to have defended the early communist idea of socialization even of marriage and the family, a point which seems to have become obsolete in the twentieth century. This again shows that it is always necessary to insist on a precise definition of goals wherever socialism or communism is being advocated.

We have said that socialism and communism hardly differ at all in terms of the meaning of the words. However, they have been given different meanings by different schools of thought. In the imprecise way the two terms have generally been used during the last hundred years, socialism has come to be understood as the less radical version of social reform. Communism, in contrast, is thought of as an all-encompassing ideology, often associated with the use of violence for the achievement of its goals. The two terms are often loosely identified with the two historical streams of the labor movement: socialism with social democracy and communism with Marxism-Leninism. (This distinction, however, is not universally accepted, as can be seen from the fact that historians speak of the communism of the early church [Acts 4:32] but not of its socialism.)

Another differentiation of the two terms is to be found in Marxism itself. Here the two terms seem to be defined by their arrangement in historical sequence. After the revolution that is envisaged, society will go through a period of socialism. At this stage the socialization of the means of production and the collectivization of other forms of life are successively implemented. At this stage, however, the contradiction between socialized life and the alienation caused by such phenomena as the division of labor, forms of social hierarchy and the state itself, has not yet been abolished. These will be abolished only in communism, the phase of history in which peace, justice, the new type of man and the new society will finally be established.

Now, in terms of political economy, Marxism is only one form of socialism-communism. There have been many other forms of socialism and communism before, besides and after Marx. But Marxism goes far beyond the economic aspects. It is an all-encompassing system of thinking and living, a total conception of the world and humanity. In other words, Marxism is an *ideology*, world view *(Weltanschauung)* and an agenda which provides the individual with answers in every sphere of life and which denies the validity of alternative answers in every sphere as well. This is why the French sociologist Jules Monnerot felt inclined to describe Marxism as a "new Islam," that is, as a religion which, if necessary, will be spread by use of the sword.[5]

Indeed, Marxism shows a number of characteristics

which indicate that it has to be understood as a kind of "religion," a basic and overall obligation. Marxism is, if you will allow the paradox, a secular religion, for it undertakes to reveal the meaning of life to its adherents and simultaneously demands their full commitment. Other observers have interpreted Marxism as a heretical form of Christianity. Indeed, Marxism includes several doctrines which formally resemble Christian dogmatics. It has a creation doctrine of its own, that is, a doctrine of the genesis of the world and humanity, as well as a doctrine of some kind of original sin (the division of labor) from which the whole of humanity is still suffering. Marxism affirms a pronounced doctrine of salvation which includes belief in a redeemer of mankind, namely the proletariat. It moreover has a doctrine of the church, which is an association of the first fruits of the new mankind (the Party). Finally, it holds a doctrine of the so-called last things, a doctrine of the purpose and aim of history, an eschatology which, though not developed in detail, is proclaimed with emphasis.

Marxism is nothing less than a program for creating a new humanity and a new world in which all present conflicts will be solved, a world in which humanity will totally rule over nature and at the same time be totally reconciled to it. To shape a society of—paradoxically—total individual freedom and, at the same time, the complete realization of communal life, is the aim of Marxism.

One cannot go far wrong in assuming that Marxism is a secularized vision of the kingdom of God. It is the kingdom of man. The race will at last undertake to create for itself that "new earth in which righteousness dwells" (2 Pet. 3:13). For too long religion has been unable to grant humanity the realization on earth of this lifelong dream. So man himself has taken over.

Understanding Marxism as a secularized form of the battle for the realization of God's kingdom will also best explain its double claim of an all-encompassing theory and a passionate practice. The famous if somewhat heterodox Marxist, Ernst Bloch, in this very sense talked of the human "assumption of power."[6] Toward this end Marxists will work with "cool scientific analysis" and at the same time "glowing enthusiasm."[7]

There is another angle to the question, what is Marxism? As we quote Bloch we must be aware of Marxist schools in the West which present Marxism as a cool, strictly emotionless socio-political theory, thus reducing Karl Marx's teaching to a socialist economic policy. Here neither moral judgment and indignation over the social misery of the proletariat of the nineteenth century nor the utopian element, the promise of a better world, is taken to represent a basic motif for Marx. Marxism is nothing but a scientific analysis of the laws of social development. This, it is said, was exactly the scope of, for example, Engels's treatise *Socialism: Utopian and Scientific* (1880).

It is significant, however, that this book belongs to a late period of Engels's life. Engels was set on the road leading to Marxism by some clearly emotional experiences; the conflict with his father, a Christian factory owner, played a major role.

Marx's essays also did not lack emotion. In his first major published essay proclaiming Communism, which has the somewhat abstract title (belied by the fervor of the article itself) "A Contribution to the Critique of Hegel's Philosophy of Right: Introduction" (1844), Marx expressly speaks of "indignation."[8] And even before that time, in his last article written from a liberal standpoint ("Debates on the Law on Thefts of Wood," 1842), Marx voices the humanist protest—the exasperation at and condemnation of the manipulation of the law by landowners and the so-called Christian state.[9]

Even the coolest technicians of revolution usually have crossed their Rubicons with similar motivations. For instance, Lenin's decision for the revolution was influenced by his hatred of the system which had destroyed his revered older brother. There is a basic emotional decision presupposed all the way, even if it later becomes emotion which is controlled so it does not get into the way of shrewd calculation.

Every revolution needs emotional motivation. The Communists prove this today. Otherwise there would be no reason for the programmed preaching of hatred against the class enemy. A merely academic form of Marxism could never hope to kindle a mass movement; it certainly was not the kind of Marxism that fascinated students in years past. Rather, the appeal of Marxism, its advertising and recruiting power, rose from a humanist impulse which cannot even be fully rationalized. True, Marxism for the first hundred years of its existence mainly stressed its materialism, but today strangely enough its propaganda maximizes its inherently idealistic element. Without this, one could not understand the renewal of Marxist influence in—of all places—the affluent society and among the children of the bourgeoisie. Marxism appeals to the middle class not because the people are struggling for basic necessities, but because they are seeking some meaning for life.

There is a deeper reason for this dispute over the reduction of Marxism to economics. Today we find very differing concepts of Marxism among those who claim to be Marxists. While "orthodox" Marxists insist on retaining the whole inherited content of the doctrine of Marx, Engels and Lenin, including its perspective of the future, others wish to take the works of Karl Marx merely as a "living philosophical inspiration" and demand the liberty to "develop Marxism in the sense that Karl Marx himself would have intended." They are the "revisionists." Marxists, it seems, are divided along the same lines as theology: orthodox and liberal, dogmatists and reformers.

For the analysis of Marxism, however, it is vital to realize that the orthodox faction is in power while the "liberals," as far as they come from countries in the Communist bloc, have mostly left and gone to the West.

Therefore, for our present discussion of Marxism it would be both unrealistic and misleading to present Marxism in a form which may be only the conception of an individual Marxist author colored by his personal predilections, a conception which is politically and historically irrelevant. Rather, we must deal with those forms of Marxism which, though possibly less beloved, nevertheless claim historical authenticity and represent a power of the first order. We shall have to deal with the entirety of Marxism, which includes its atheism, anthropology, eschatological promise and so forth.

Because Marxism is this all-encompassing program of the dominion of man, it acquires the character of an alternative to the Christian faith which is centered on the dominion of God. The prophets, the Lord and his apostles all bring the good news of a kingdom of peace and justice in which God himself governs, a kingdom fully realized only in the future but growing and present also within history. In Christianity, too, the promise contains the creation of a new world and a new humanity, though only through an act of God himself.

Therefore, we seem to find a certain similarity of aims. But with the consistent denial of God in Marxism, there is also a thoroughgoing contrast. Given this presupposition, Christians should not expect to be able to assimilate or adapt Christianity to Marxism and its ends. Admittedly, one of the traditional weaknesses of Christians has been the tendency to look to the successful movements and ruling ideas of the day and to find themselves at least in partial harmony with them. This tendency could already be seen in the Old Testament, but it is also the problem of each generation of the Christian church.

Today gods from the right and the left compete to impress the church and persuade it, causing it to reduce itself to nothing but the moderate expression of the accepted opinions of the day. In contrast to this the first task of the church is to find and keep its identity. Profile helps orientation. Marxism always stresses the partisanism of its thinking, and this helps to clarify it for others. In the same way Christians must begin with a basis of allegiance to the biblical Jesus and the apostolic faith, which is no longer open for dispute. Christians can presuppose, just as much as the Marxists do, that the truth is already given and does not need to be discovered in the dialogue.

Although we recognize the essential dissimilarity of Christianity and Marxism, it does not follow that Christians have nothing to learn from studying Marxism. John Wesley used to say he was willing to learn from anyone. Even if Christianity were merely a human movement vis-à-vis Marxism, we would remind ourselves that in business competitors gain by studying the other's strengths in order to remedy the weaknesses in themselves. Surely with regard to the contents of faith, Christians will not expect anything new from the encounter with Marxism. But concerning the forms of human commitment to a given purpose, our study of others, including Marxists, may help us to further understand our own weaknesses and ineffectiveness. Ultimately, of course, we are measured only by the standards of the faith.

Chapter 2

The Challenges of Marxism

We have said that Christians can understand some of their own weaknesses better through studying Marxism. There are four major points at which Marxism confronts Christianity and issues a challenge. These have to do with our knowledge of truth, our practice of the faith, our view of reality and the purpose we see in life. We will look at each of these in turn.

Knowledge of Truth
In Marxism we observe the quiet presupposing of a precise knowledge of justice, freedom and human dignity; in short, of truth. It is these presuppositions which allow Marxists at any time to speak firmly, categorically and with the claim of infallibility: "This is it. This, and nothing else!"

Around 1968 when in the universities all traditional Christian and social standards had been cast into doubt by the roaming postulate of pluralism, the Marxists used to say that pluralism of conviction is the most despicable thing imaginable. In the midst of pervasive relativism, Marxists began to affirm positive statements and to lead the public mind in their own direction. One Christian student lamented: "What a miserable situation to be in! Only the Communists still dare to state things in the affirmative. The Christians, like so many others, now talk in relative terms: 'We are merely asking questions. We do not have the solution either.' " The knowledge of truth as something which can be clearly distinguished from its opposite and which is not just a matter of individual opinion seemed to have been lost. Marxists, however, did have definite convictions—a stated standard of justice—and they were almost the only ones who did.

Furthermore, the agenda of Marxism does not end with a statement of truth. It is a characteristic of Marxism to turn the presupposed standard of truth critically against existing reality. Admittedly, Marx speaks about developing the truth from reality itself. But that does not mean that the result of this developmental process should not again be passionately set against reality as what should be is contrasted with what is. This mood of confrontation creates the pathos of Marxism: We break with the world as it is. Our actions are measured by a world as it should be. Thence comes the protest against the here and now.

In 1843, at the age of twenty-five, Karl Marx wrote to Arnold Ruge, a one-time liberal comrade: "For our part, we must expose the old world to the full light of day and shape the new one in a positive way."[1] The task was characterized as "ruthless criticism of the existing order, ruthless in that it will shrink neither from its own discoveries nor from conflict with the powers that be."[2] Marxism demands a critique of conditions, that is, of existing reality, through confrontation with "true reality" and with Marxism's final convictions concerning the true nature of humanity. Criticism is always the application to an object of a standard assumed beforehand. In 1844 in his keynote essay, "Contribution to the Critique of Hegel's Philosophy of Right: Introduction," Marx exclaims: War on conditions in Germany! They are beneath the level of humanity.[3] He implies that he knows what that level of humanity should be. Marx presupposes truth, and he turns it critically against a reality that does not match it.

Christian truth. The challenge then to Christians is this: What is truth for Christendom? Confronted by Marxism, Christians have to ask themselves: Do we still believe in truth, or are we content with a pot full of relativities? What would we be willing to be taken to task for? Do we dare to affirm anything? Is Christian faith the truth to which we are committed? Is there still anything we would state categorically? Or do we agree when some people reduce the contents of Christianity to a history of particular religious opinions?

Most importantly, we must ask: Do we as Christians also have a truth which critically turns against rotten reality? Or is the truth of Christianity a dormant truth from which nothing follows? Is it truth of an otherworldly nature only which, due to its very essence, could never confront reality on earth because it was never meant to?

These questions immediately expose the dangerous tendency of orthodox theology to view the truth simply as some heavenly system of thought which does not throw any light on existing conditions and does not try to change them.

Under the influence of the passionate critique wielded by Marxism, we may remember that in Scripture there is not a single truth that is not intended to be a call addressed to mankind.

Within biblical revelation the call to repentance is given a place similar to that of criticism in the Marxist philosophy. This means that it is not conditions, but first men and women who need to change, who cannot remain as they are. A call to repentance, too, is a confrontation between that which should be and that which is, a demand for change in persons and conditions. In preaching repentance the prophets called the people of God back to their true destiny. And when Jesus said that "the Son of man came to seek and to save the lost" (Lk. 19:10), he was presupposing a silent judgment on a wrongful state of affairs. At the same time, however, Jesus' proclamation expressed his resolve to help change that which is not as it should be. He resembles not the critical government health officer demanding higher standards of health, but a surgeon conferring it on a patient.

Marx's truth and Christ's. Whoever as a Christian listens to the message of Marxism will be reminded that Christ has not asked us to accommodate ourselves to disease, to existing evil conditions, to sin in our lives or in the community, but to work for change and bring healing. We are not to abandon the world and the human race to evil, but to become the salt of the earth to keep human society from decay.

It would seem, then, that in Christianity, as in Marxism, some kind of truth is the standard for measuring the rightness (justice) in the world. This seeming similarity does not imply, however, that the contents of truth in Marxism and Christianity are the same.

Nor are the ways and means which truth will use to exercise its critical function identical. Although the cleavage between the way things are and the way they should be is just as painful to Christians as to Marxists, Marx's terms —such as "indignation," "denunciation," "criticism," "combat," "war,"[4] and violent turnover of existing conditions—do not fit Christ's attitudes and actions. Rather, in pointing out how Christ dealt with sinners we see that Christians too will handle the cleavage in other ways than Marxists. So the ways and means will be different.

Nevertheless, Christians should clearly be as grieved by

the distance between what ought to be and what is as Marx was by the disjuncture between what he saw as truth and the conditions of his day.

Truth in Action
Not only does Marx presuppose knowledge of the truth, not only does he push its critical application (which could still be a theoretical occupation), but he also demands a commitment to the practical realization of the truth. The task is not only to recognize the "truth of this world" as opposed to some truth remaining beyond, but to realize and establish, set up and enforce the "truth of this world."[5]

With this Marx raises the question of the relation between theory and practice. The impulse of Marxist ideology is not only theoretical, but practical. This is made clear early in Marx's critique of the traditional attitude of speculative philosophy. In contrast to Feuerbach, his immediate predecessor in the history of German philosophy, Marx does not limit himself to lifting the philosophy of idealism from its hinges by means of philosophy. Rather, Marx asserts in his famous Thesis XI concerning Feuerbach: "The philosophers have only *interpreted* the world in various ways; the point is to *change* it."[6] Until now, he says, changes always took place on the level of interpretation and theory, but that is not enough. Surely Marx was sufficiently confident of his skills as a philosopher to believe that he could add to the number of existing interpretations of the world a new, superior one. What he asked for, however, was not a changed interpretation of the world, but a change of the world itself! This insight led Marx to organize the international workers' movement. Practice will also finally decide the value of a theory.

Does faith demand action? Marx's attitude to practice is so well known that we need not go into it further. As Christians, however, it forces us to deal with the question of whether our theory demands practice, whether our faith insists on action. This question again has to be asked on two levels: on the level of theory and on the level of practice.

On the first level, we ask if faith, according to its very nature, should call forth action. Ought it to turn to practice? Or does believing only connote thought, understanding, opinion, interpretation of life, assent, acknowledgment—something which is the task of our intellects or perhaps our tongues?

In the Bible it is clear that faith does not begin and end in thought. It must result in action. Jesus told his disciples: "If you know these things [that is, that they ought to wash one another's feet], blessed are you if you do them" (Jn. 13:17; compare Mt. 7:24).

Has faith produced action? If we agree that Christianity should determine practical life, immediately the second, more painful part of the question appears: *Does it* actually do so? Does our faith in fact generate those actions it should generate?

Confrontation with Marxism and its demand for practice forces Christians to recall the famous but easily forgotten words of our Lord: "If any one chooses to do God's will, he will find out whether my teaching comes from God or whether I speak on my own" (Jn. 7:17 NIV). This means nothing less than that the proper understanding of Christ's message can only be reached by practically doing God's will: Christ's truth can never be assessed adequately on the level of theory.

There are some traditions within Protestantism which take that statement of Christ and immediately encase and neutralize it. It is hardly ever mentioned, or it is supposed to be problematic, even perhaps stemming from some ancient source alien to the gospel. When John 7:17 was quoted in a discussion between theologians recently, a participant remarked: "Oh, that's the darling verse of Ritschlian [that is, liberal] theology." This observation seemed to be enough to disqualify any argument based on the verse. Nevertheless, it was not Ritschl but Christ himself who spoke those words, and it was Christ who also said, "Not every one who says to me, 'Lord, Lord,' shall enter the kingdom of heaven, but he who does the will of my Father who is in heaven" (Mt. 7:21). This is the point which lies behind Christ's criticism of the scribes and Pharisees. To the people, Jesus said, "The scribes and the Pharisees sit on Moses' seat; so practice and observe whatever they tell you, but not what they do; for they preach, but do not practice" (Mt. 23:2-3).

Paul, praising the gift of divine grace more than anybody else, nevertheless teaches in the same vein as Christ: "For we must all appear before the judgment seat of Christ, so that each one may receive good or evil, according to what he has done in the body" (2 Cor. 5:10). *Done in the body* is a phrase which clearly denotes the objective realm of practice.

James also makes this point with regard to the relationship of rich and poor in a congregation. Particularly here everything depends on practice, not on sentiment and kind words only: "If a brother or sister is ill-clad and in lack of daily food, and one of you says to them, 'Go in peace, be warmed and filled,' without giving them the things needed for the body, what does it profit?" From this James concludes this general rule: "So faith by itself, if it has no works, is dead" (Jas. 2:15-17). We might put it this way: Faith not resulting in action is superfluous.

A history of failure. Although the testimony of the New Testament is clear enough, it has been dimmed within some Protestant theological traditions—possibly for reasons of an ancient and now almost irrational antagonism to Roman Catholicism and its alleged idea of salvation by works. Protestantism, with regard to faith's need for practice, retains a deep-seated uncertainty. In theology we still suffer under the pressure of a tradition which was quite outspoken during the Reformation and which made it possible for leading men of the Protestant church to pronounce statements like "Good works are not only not useful, but detrimental to salvation" (because pride would certainly be roused by them).[7]

Since the Reformation, every century has seen theological traditions which have tried to neutralize in the most ingenious ways the biblical imperative to practice the faith. Adolf Schlatter, the great exegete of the first half of the twentieth century and one of the rare personalities in the history of theology who did not submit to the rule of dogmatic traditions because he felt bound by Scripture, termed this problem of practice "the weakness of ethics in Protestantism."[8]

So what are we to do? In meeting the practical orientation of Marxism, will we boldly affirm Christianity's essentially theoretical character and thereby support the Marxist claim that the Christian faith is a form of idealism? Or will we allow ourselves to be challenged and criticized by the Marxist concept, recognizing that while it does not touch the source of the Christian faith, it affects some of our traditions? Could it help us to see that we must—and can—liberate ourselves from these traditions and go back to the source?

The Real and the Unreal

The Marxist insistence on concrete reality as the theater of human life poses the same question from another angle. Practice and reality are related categories.

In one of their first books Marx and Engels identified their stance as "real humanism." In *The Holy Family* they wrote: "The first proposition of profane socialism rejects emancipation *in mere theory* as an illusion and for *real* freedom it demands besides the idealistic '*will*,' very tangible, very material conditions."[9] They argued with their former philosopher friend Bruno Bauer about how the decisive liberation of humanity was to take place: in theory through the mediation of some new insight, new vision or change in consciousness; or in the practical and material conditions of human life. Marx and Engels saw this antithesis in the situation of the industrial labor force in Europe: "These ... workers, employed, for instance, in the Manchester or Lyons workshops, do not believe that by 'pure thinking' they will be able to argue away their industrial masters and their own practical debasement. They are most painfully aware of the *difference* between *being* and *thinking,* between *consciousness* and *life.* They know that property, capital, money, wage-labour and the like are no ideal figments of the brain but very practical, very objective products of their self-estrangement and that therefore they must be abolished in a practical and objective way for man to become man not only in *thinking,* in *consciousness,* but in mass *being,* in life."[10]

Is Christianity real? This attack leveled by Marx and Engels is of special concern to Christians because the slogan "real humanism," which sums up the attack, was also used to point out the alleged unreality of Christian theology. "Real humanism" was the battle cry shouted at the thin spiritualism of contemporary Protestant theology as well as at speculative, idealistic philosophy. Both of these never got anywhere near the actual situation of the proletariat, because they were so occupied with more spiritual things. Therefore, Marx and Engels looked at this kind of "religious inhumanity" as one of their main enemies.[11]

For the moment we shall not deal with the question of whether their assumptions about nineteenth-century theology were right or wrong. More important than a judgment on some random historical trend in Christian theology is the question: How are things today in this respect? Is Christendom today influenced by the same tradition which formed theology in the nineteenth century? Does it continue to produce the same damaging effects?

With a view to self-criticism Christians need to ask what kind of reality we ascribe to God's saving work in Jesus Christ. What sphere of reality is it? Where does it take place? Sin, the alienation from God which is analogous to the concept of self-alienation for Marx and Engels, apparently has objective reality. The Bible certainly treats the subject as though it is a real, objective matter which needs to be dealt with in an objective and practical manner.

Just as the destruction through sin of relationships among people and between people and God is not merely theoretical, so the redeeming action of Christ is not something merely thought up; it is not the theoretical communication of some doctrine or otherworldly decision of God. In order to make good for human sin Christ on the cross died a bloody death. The imprinting of this event on the life of his followers must take just as concrete a shape. Indeed it is a painful and costly process, as evidenced in the conversions of Peter, Paul, Zacchaeus and the "woman ... who was a sinner" (Lk. 7:37). All of them not only believed that there had been a change in God's heavenly judgment upon them, but they also lived out the change in their attitudes, their use of property and so forth. Thus, the new birth was not and is not simply a change in status before God but an alteration in one's entire earthly being. In addition, what has just been said about the reality of the new birth must also be said about the concreteness of the ongoing process of sanctification.

"Unreal" theology. A dominant stream of theological thinking, under whose influence mainstream theology still stands today, has nevertheless taught the opposite. Within this tradition the quest for reality (which at least in the encounter with Marxism is crucial) is being rejected. Stressing God's justifying judgment and thereby neglecting the factual renewal of the sinner is an old disease in Protestant theology, especially the German theology that has often set the trend for large areas of the world. To this day certain forms of theology lack the balance of justification and sanctification which is the heritage of Calvin, and the strong emphasis on the ethics of the creation order which is added in Scandinavian Lutheranism.

Furthermore, two theologies which have been influential during the last two generations have had a devastating effect in this respect. These are the "dialectical
theology" of the young Karl Barth and Rudolf Bultmann's
kerygma theology. Under the impression made by atheist
scientists from the beginning of the century, both aimed
at a deobjectification of theology. In his "dialectical"
years, Karl Barth was not only at odds with, but openly
rejected the quest for reality and the objective world which
Karl Marx made every attempt to reach. Bultmann, with
his theory of the Christian faith as a new understanding
of self, added to the effect and made Christianity a matter
of individual, private thinking. The effect of the theologies of Bultmann and the early Barth was to withdraw
faith from the open field of reality, where it might be
critically destroyed by secularism, by making the object of
faith either completely internal or transcendent. The
world, society, the outward actions necessary for human
beings, all objective reality then remains empty of God and
of God's work in and through humanity.

On the kingdom of God, the central notion of the Christian faith, Barth wrote around 1930 that he had now understood the "real other-worldly meaning" of the phrase.[12]
If this was the whole truth, it must be utterly inappropriate
for Christians to hope to experience something of the new
life on earth or to feel called to help forward its realization through obedience and suffering. Bultmann sec-
onded this by proposing that Christianity was above all
withdrawal from the world; that is, otherworldliness,
spiritualization.

It is striking to see how these theologians immediately
fall under the critique of Marx. They again have only
"interpreted" man in a different way, but, as Marx said,
"the point is to change him."[13]

Does this spiritualization of Christianity have anything
to do with the rise of Marxism? We have reason to believe that the early rise of Marxism in the first half of

the nineteenth century was encouraged by a theology and piety that was indifferent to human needs. It was interested in the soul of man only, not in the conditions of his physical existence. Spiritualism is a central notion in the theology of Schleiermacher, who was then the influential voice. And Engels accused the pietism of the nineteenth century of spiritual exodus from the industrial world into the ghetto of the pious.[14]

The consequences of irrelevance. Today Marxism welcomes theological irrelevance because it makes Marxism look good. When theology fails to confront the real current issues, Marxism moves in to offer its atheist solutions.[15] This is the first consequence of "unreal" theology.

In recent years theologians have begun to doubt the wisdom of overspiritualizing the faith. They have seen the result: Christianity is divorced from everyday life. Those who have been awakened by the Marxist demand for reality and have become aware of these developments within theology and their disastrous consequences, will no longer be satisfied with reductionist theological traditions. They will look afresh for the effects of God's work in history, and they will find confidence for the shaping of today's reality. We can respond the same way one theology student did to those who present us with an irrelevant gospel, "If the gospel does not change my life, I'll drop it."

There is another consequence of the theological exodus from reality. It creates the widespread arbitrariness in ethics and social concern from which today's Protestantism suffers. We are largely unprepared for the social problems encircling us. If our faith has little to do with the world around us, then we must hastily borrow ethical ideas from elsewhere, from liberal humanism or from socialism. We should, however, rid ourselves of our ideological enslavement and aim at social ethics of our own—not exclusively Christian, because it has to fit a pluralist society, but consonant with our faith. We urgently need biblically informed doctrines of property, of the organization of work, and of the different modes of God's government. In order to develop them we first must divest ourselves of the unreal notion of God—a notion which fails to take account of the concrete ordering, leading and acting of he who is really there and is not silent.

Purpose for Life

Another challenge to Christians resulting from Marxism is the question of aim or purpose. Marxism characteristically and consciously understands its truths as aims to be achieved.[16] Every Marxist is aware of the aims of Marxism and will readily explain them to outsiders. Marxists know what their job is and they do it.

If someone has a purpose, his or her actions will be goal-oriented and single-minded. A purpose provides an organizing center for all of one's actions. A goal in life provides "a point from which to lift the world off its hinges." Lenin is said to have stated: "The revolutionary spirit expresses itself not so much in violent methods as in the fact that each single action of every day is related to the whole." It is the aim which makes Marxism such an all-encompassing concept of human existence, an *ideology*. It is, as Eduard Spranger, one of Europe's great philosophers and educators, says, "Something to believe in, to live for and to sacrifice for."[17] It is this dedication to a cause which confers on Marxism that conspicuous missionary zeal.

The possession of an overall aim will do much for the life of an individual. In recent years there has been much publicity about the younger generation's search for a purpose in life. The rise of countless religious cults is evidence of this desire for direction. But it is not just the youth who feel a need for purpose. We also hear frequently about middle-aged people experiencing a "midlife" crisis when they realize that their highest career goals have been missed or achieved without producing a feeling of satisfaction. With a true purpose a person's life receives new meaning. He or she discovers a task worth performing for reasons beyond the craving for private happiness.

Wolfgang Leonhard, one of the best-trained young Party intellectuals of Eastern Europe who defected to the West in the fifties, described what it meant to have a purpose in life when he related this story from his two years at the Komintern (Party) College in the Soviet Union. He recalls a little speech given to the students by the director of the school, a man called Mikhailov:

He spoke of the dangers and the splendours of revolutionary life. At the end of his brief address, he took a box of matches out of his pocket. "Perhaps," he said, "the best way I can make clear my thoughts and feelings at this moment is by a concrete example."

With that, he took out a match, and struck it. The match burned out in a few seconds, leaving only a little ash behind. Mikhailov looked at us amiably and a little thoughtfully.

"Isn't the life of an ordinary man just like that? He gives out a little flame at first, and then a bigger flame, and finally burns out. All that remains is a little useless ash. Man lives, works, establishes a family, brings children into the world, dies and is mourned at best by the members of his family and a few of his friends: a futile, superfluous life. When we look at our own life by contrast—a life of experience, danger, travel, imprisonment; with responsible tasks, with membership of the great family which we call 'the Party,' with a clear and firm objective as the cornerstone of a new world, with countless comrades to mourn us at our death—is that not something very, very different from the futility of a spent match?"

We were all enthralled. Never before had anyone at the school spoken to us like this.

Mikhailov looked attentively at us, at each one in turn. "You may think on what I have said, now and

then, perhaps," he said, *"especially when you are in difficulties. It helps."* [18]
A kingdom for a purpose! Indeed. But we would be wrong if we concluded that this is a matter for some ambitious elite only, that anyone could just as well live a confident and meaningful life without such a horizon. On the contrary, every man and woman needs a framework for orientation to and interpretation of life, they need an answer to the question of meaning which is posed by life itself if they are to avoid nihilism and spiritual death. Without aim and commitment no man can exist in the long run.

That this is not only a matter of individual taste or preference, but a necessity for survival, is explained by a consideration which I owe to the late philosopher and physician Wilhelm Kütemeyer of the University of Heidelberg. Talking to the American sociologist Eugen Rosenstock-Huessy, Kütemeyer raised the question which tortured so many members of Germany's younger generation: What sort of breakdown within German society and especially among the elite allowed the rise of National Socialism? The two men concluded that it began decades before the rise of Hitler when German intellectuals had in large numbers thrown aside the Christian faith as a binding purpose and a life-changing commitment. You could be a Christian or not be a Christian, and the latter was slightly more elegant. Then, after years of meaninglessness and lack of orientation, there came a hunger for commitment and a thirst for something to believe in. As they had despised the Living Water, people now grasped the next available offer to quench the thirst, and that was the ideology of Nazism. So they swallowed the poison and destroyed their lives and the lives of so many innocent people around them.

People cannot live consistent lives as nihilists, having nothing to live for but themselves.

The artistic task. We find proof of the truth of this last statement in the lives of prominent writers today. Unlike most of their fellow citizens who make their living by fulfilling objective work orders, authors (and artists generally) in their work in part reproduce their own subjectivity. Also, free-lance artists need to make a name for themselves in order to be able to make a living. This higher egotism inherent in the artist's task (an egotism which can reveal itself in quite vulgar forms) frequently leads to the demand for absolute liberty for the individual and to the liquidation of objective norms. At this point, the artist's energies, if not given direction, begin to dissolve. Nihilism will put an end to all artistic production if an aim is not found which again can focus the artist's energies and make possible the discipline and concentration required for the artistic task.

Some of the best-known authors of our time, drifting in the bottomless sea of nihilism, grasped the ideology of Marxism in the hope that its aims would bring their artistic energy to focus on some worthwhile goal. They form an impressive array. Let us look at a few of them.

Bertolt Brecht, the famous Communist playwright, in his early years (as even the most careful and sympathetic biographers make us understand), lived a life of unscrupulous egotism. All the world around him, be it inanimate objects or human flesh, became a tool for the development and satisfaction of his artistic individuality.[19] But it soon dawned on him that even within a program of ruthless self-realization there is a battle for supremacy between the senses and the mind. When Brecht embraced Marxism as a concern demanding commitment in the mid-1920s, he experienced a great sense of relief as though he'd been saved from a battle unto death. He saluted collectivism as the victory—both personally and socially—over those divergent individual interests which, according to Karl Marx, are the essence of the bourgeois as well as obviously the essence of the artistic existence.[20]

We find the very same development in the life of the

famous French philosopher and writer, Jean Paul Sartre. As we read *The Words*, the autobiography of his early years, we discover that the demand for self-realization and self-determination is the all-embracing theme.[21] Consequently, his appearance in the 1940s as a philosopher is characterized by a demand for absolute individual liberty. This rejection of higher values then created the desert from which he turned to an unconditional support for Marxism, including the glorification of Stalinism.

The life of the eminent playwright and novelist, Peter Weiss, author of several plays, including *The Persecution and Assassination of Jean Marat*, exhibits the same pattern. His autobiographic novels from before his conversion to Marxism in 1963, all show a person constantly occupied with himself and battling to find his identity as an artist. His surroundings, people included, seemingly only existed as if behind a veil, although he did not exploit them with the same impertinence as did Brecht. His ego was the center around which everything revolved. Only in a few instances did he experience something like a bad conscience (for example, when he met a Communist who spent his life working for the progress of humanity and not merely for his own agenda of self-discovery and fulfillment).[22]

After his conversion to Marxism in 1963, Weiss stated that the effect of aimlessness in the West was to destroy at the root all cultural and creative activity. "Literature in the bourgeois countries," he said, "develops towards anarchism for lack of obligation."[23] He said he had finally felt unable to reconcile his lack of purpose with self-esteem.

A final example in this series of star authors who embraced Communism is depicted by novelist Martin Walser in his 1973 novel *Die Gallistl'sche Krankheit (The Gallistl Disease)*. With painful intensity, Walser describes the growing despair of an author who looks into himself to find something worth saying. The more tense and strained he becomes, the less he can produce. This concentration on the ego and its reduction to something like a mathematical point leads to a time when the meaninglessness of his life is revealed in that he begins to go insane. At this point, however, a few Communist friends gently lead the sick man out of his self-imposed prison and give him back to life. The book does not end with a triumphant fanfare for Communism, but with an awakened admiration for people who live for some great cause, rather than for themselves.[24]

In 1975 Peter Weiss, mentioned previously, published the first part of a large novel entitled *The Aesthetics of Resistance.* This is a Marxist educational novel describing the development of the Marxist ideal in the education of a young person. In this model biography Weiss reveals some of the things which he himself believes to have found in embracing Marxism. Three significant elements stand out: a consciousness of history, a principle for action and a sense of belonging. All three together make life meaningful.

Through the aim of world revolution Weiss's hero finds the ability to interpret each moment of history as well as the present from one homogenous point of view. This enables him to interpret and control both the past and present. And it simultaneously shows him his meaningful place in life. In principle, he no longer will be confused about what is to be done next because he has learned to see each moment in history in relation to the revolutionary goal. Added to this is the consciousness of being part of a world movement which is expected to win final victory. This perspective appears several times in Weiss's book: "Although only at the beginning of my journey, it had become clear to me that we would nowhere be at home except in our partisanship. . . . In our political decision we had found our sense of belonging."[25] The homeless individual ego of the artist found the haven of the collective.

The cost of commitment. There is much to be gained in

communion, in union with a cause. But there is also much to be given up. The last chapter of Martin Esslin's book on Brecht carries the intriguing title, "Pitfalls of Commitment." It recounts the price which Brecht had to pay for the aim he had been given during his Communist career.[26] This high price to be paid for a manmade purpose comes to light in Peter Weiss's book too. Almost everything which the young Marxist featured in Weiss's book set out to find later he loses to Communism. Obedience to a party line which may not always be understood or inwardly accepted takes the place of freedom. Party hierarchy replaces equality. Fraternity is pushed aside by the continuous battle for supremacy of individual interpretations of dogma, interpretations which become the tools individuals use to fight for personal supremacy.

Because Marxists have pledged their allegiance to the motto, "The end justifies the means," they must be ready to deny even their strongest personal convictions. That motto results in some people ruling over the rest—people who have the right to interpret the situation and, respectively, to command. The battle for social justice began with individual consciences making independent moral judgments, but the continuation of that battle within Marxism requires the same consciences to be violated again and again. The price for having both an aim in life and the proud knowledge of belonging to the elite of the future consists of one's own convictions. In Weiss's book, the hero's father, a workers' leader trained in the Marxist criticism of religion, has become skeptical of the Party. He says that "the Party has become a kind of church into which the individual must dissolve."[27] Marxism is a humanism too costly.

Wolfgang Leonhard also found the manmade aim of Marxism less convincing than the director of his school had led him to believe. He went to Yugoslavia and later to the West. For him and many others, including several eminent writers, Marxism became a salvation doctrine that failed. Arthur Koestler, famed author of *Darkness at Noon*, contributed to the book *The God Who Failed* along with several other prominent writers who describe their personal experiences of disillusionment with Marxism.[28] Koestler thought that the failure of Marxism was rooted in the concept that the end justifies the means.[29]

The idea that the end justifies the means was also the primary stumbling block for Gustav Regler, one of the leading Communist commissars during the Spanish Civil War in the 1930s. He tells his story in his moving autobiography with the significant title of *The Ear of Malchus*,[30] taken from John 18:10 and Matthew 26:52 where Jesus says, "Put your sword back into its place; for all who take the sword will perish by the sword."

Willy Münzenberg, the brilliant organizer of Communist propaganda in Germany in the 1920s and one of the central figures in the German resistance movement in exile after the Nazi seizure of power, turned away from Communism when Stalin signed the pact with Hitler in 1940. To Münzenberg the Communist purpose did not justify every means, for instance, alliance with the very enemy.[31] "The end justifies the means" is the moral principle of unrestrained atheism. It will finally pervert everything, without exception, and turn everything into its opposite by even justifying those means which annihilate the purpose.

An illusory goal? There are doubts arising also over the quality of the Marxist goal. They spring up as we subject them to a closer scrutiny. As we know, Marx generally refused to describe his hopes for a Communist future in more detail. He stopped at the prediction of the revolution and the demand to change the inhuman conditions existing in society. His more explicit purposes were of an immediate character. He did not himself enlarge on detailed questions about the future. But certain questions cannot be avoided. They arise from characteristics of human nature and existence and point to a possible exclusiveness and to the illusory quality of Karl Marx's final goals.

Marx's anthropological ideal was "the rich man who is *profoundly and abundantly endowed with all his senses.*"[32] Some of today's Marxist authors render this not unevenly when they portray their concept of the meaning of life as freely chosen activity directed at developing one's individual abilities to the fullest, while being in harmony with the collective progress of history.[33] Marxism thus seems to hold up what is essentially an anthropology of the able.

It is, then, no wonder that a young generation of atheist intellectuals, who are free, gifted, talented, prone to espouse immediate causes but less concerned about the distant future, should be attracted to Marxism. Such a commitment would be further facilitated by the obvious dissolution of all previous loyalties through secularism and by the ensuing fear of total nihilism. Marxism also appeals to the strong moral consciousness of the young, a consciousness muted by secularism and suffocated by nihilism, which can find voice again in Marxism—even if only in indignant protest, criticizing what *others* do wrongly.

Nevertheless, the questions remain: What does Marxism offer those who just are not endowed with many natural talents, such as a high intellectual awareness and an ability for discernment? What about those who have been rendered inactive by life, who are old or ill—those who can no longer hope to "give birth to human nature's inner wealth"[34] and become the rich and fully developed persons Marx promised for the future? And then, there is the problem of death and dying. Orthodox Marxist philosophers have had little to say on this subject. This may be an indication that Marxism does not yield an answer for individual death which after all is an essential characteristic of human existence with which everyone has to come to terms.[35]

The quest for purpose. We have looked at the formal concept of aim or purpose. Yes, we need an aim and a meaning for life. But it would have to be an aim different from the aim of Marxism. In order for a purpose to help heal the contradictions of human existence, it must point beyond humanity and it must be beyond human manipulation. Manmade goals stand in danger of ignoring the human limitations which they cannot do away with, and thus becoming destructive. In the quest for purpose, humanity needs an alternative to Marxism.

A kingdom for an aim! Peter Weiss, when seeking the saving shore of a purpose, seems never to have thought of the possibility of Christianity. Why? Isn't Christianity supposed to be such a purpose, "something to believe in, to live for, and to sacrifice for"? Wolfgang Leonhard's Communist teacher spoke of "a life of experience, danger, travel, imprisonment; . . . [including] membership of the great family . . . with a clear and firm objective, as the cornerstone of a new world." Does this not bring to mind an image of Paul, the emissary of Jesus Christ? This then is the challenge which the Marxist demand for purposeful living poses to Christians: Is our faith the focus of our life—the central point to which all actions are related every day? Is that how we understand Christianity? Are we conscious of the historic task given to us, the same way Marxists are conscious of their task? Or do Christians suffer from a lack of such an awareness? Have we lost the missionary conviction and zeal which characterized the early church? In the terms of Peter Weiss: Does Christianity provide us with an understanding of the meaning of history? Does it give us a vision, a direction for action and a sense of belonging?

Christians need to find their purpose and horizon again, and they need to publicize it. They owe it to those large numbers of people who today suffer from a feeling that life is meaningless. These people cannot hope to find the answer to nihilism in a godless solution. Christians must with all their might show how life in Christ has a meaning and purpose beneficial to all humanity. They must demonstrate where the true motives for justice and reconciliation come from.

Christians must not be taken in by the myth that selfish individuals can form a universally unselfish collective. This may come about temporarily by force, but it will soon fall apart or it will be limited to superficial levels. Christians also should not allow others to mythologize social problems so that they become mysteries which others must solve. Christians must develop their own social ethics while emphasizing the need for a rebirth of humanity. Society is made up of concrete individual persons and concrete personal relationships, and Christ remains competent for the restoration of both individuals and relationships—the basic elements of society.

More than anything else, Christians need to find a new and passionate commitment to their God-given purpose. Heart and mind cannot remain empty. They need to be filled, one way or another—the mind with comprehensive thinking, the heart with passionate commitment. Turning back to the will of God is the only solution to the problems in East and West. The power of God is the answer to the misery which the human lust for power has created.

Part II

The Marxist Critique
of Religion

Chapter 3

Marx and Religion

Before any dialogue can take place between Marxism and Christianity, we must first overcome the one major objection Marxists would raise to such a dialogue. For Marx, all religion, including Christianity, is an illusion, a fantasy created by the human mind. And no dialogue is possible with an illusion. We must demonstrate, therefore, that the Christian faith is not disqualified at the outset by being illusory. We must re-examine and secure the Christian position in the face of the Marxist critique, clearing away the rubble of prejudice surrounding the issue of religion. The critique of religion is not the decisive point of debate between Marxism and Christianity. But it nevertheless needs to be dealt with in order to refute the idea that Christianity is only a product of human imagination.

When we talk about the Marxist critique of religion, we are not here talking about the very real, practical critique of religion occurring in our time in the form of the persecution of churches and individual believers which takes place in varying degrees in Communist countries. For information on such activities, we can consult the periodical *Religion in Communist Lands* and the publications of Michael Bourdeaux's Keston College research center in England.

The Marxist critique of religion is not limited to the Communist bloc. In the East this challenge is often accompanied by harassment and physical violence, whereas in the West the struggle tends to be limited to the intellectual and spiritual realms. But the battle is no less fierce. Marxists try to capture minds because they believe that minds must be conquered before fists can be set into motion.

In replying to the Marxist critique, we shall not deal with the innumerable accusations which can be brought up based on the history of the Church. For instance, a good many critics, Communists among them, have accused the church of unthinkingly blessing the use of weapons and violence. Yet during Stalin's regime in World War 2 the Communists expected the Church to approve the use of weapons. And today according to those who espouse liberation theology, the Church must again bless weapons— those of the revolutionaries. These are significant problems, but ones which lie beyond our purposes in this chapter.

Furthermore, we shall not here try to defend Christianity against those who point an accusing finger at the "sins of the popes." The inconsistencies in the lives of prominent religious leaders have recently been publicized again in atheist publications of the East and West. If our forebears have committed sins, so have the forebears of Marxism. There is already a history of Marxist "popes" and their sins. But that is not a legitimate reply. It is never sufficient to search for shortcomings; they exist wherever people are involved. Rather, we must look at the program and intentions, counting those who fulfill them and excluding those who fail.

Therefore, in this chapter we will deal with the basic principles of the critique with which Marxism attacks the central doctrines of the Christian faith. We will not concern ourselves with Marxist attacks on Christian misrepresentations of the faith. Rather we shall begin with a discussion of the content of the Marxist critique of religion, and then consider its legitimacy and finally its limits.

The Premise of All Criticism

In 1844 Karl Marx published his essay entitled "A Contribution to the Critique of Hegel's Philosophy of Law: Introduction." Contrary to its abstract title, this piece carried significant concrete weight: It was the manifesto of early Marxism. The very first sentence contained a two-point thesis: "For Germany the *criticism of religion* is in the main complete, and criticism of religion is the premise of all criticism."[1]

Let us look first at the second half of the sentence. It reads, "Criticism of religion is the premise of all criticism." This is a pronouncement about the importance, or the *rank*, of criticism of religion within Marxist thought. The critique of religion is the prerequisite—the condition, foundation and basic element—of the entire economic, political, judicial and aesthetic critique and of all critiques which may yet come to be. This sentence postulates the central position of criticism of religion and of atheism in the Marxist world.

The assertion that the criticism of religion is the premise of all criticism is valid for Marx in terms of his biography, his methodology and his motivation. The phrase is true in the sense that atheism—in history and in Marx's life— was already a fact *before* the philosophy of dialectical materialism was born. Karl Marx was an atheist before he became a dialectical materialist.[2]

Moreover, the phrase reveals the methodological priority of atheism. For Marx the criticism of religion became the methodological prerequisite for all other criticism, be it the philosophical critique of Hegel[3] or the critique of economics. There is proof to show that even in his major work of later years, *Das Kapital* (volume 1 published 1867), he used some of the same categories which he had developed in his early studies in the critique of religion.

Finally, the statement, "Criticism of religion is the premise of all criticism" has a third meaning. It indicates that the critique of religion also represents the motive, the incentive necessary for all other criticism. Marx once wrote, "The more man puts into God, the less he retains in himself."[4] This shows how much Marx felt that the elimination of religion was necessary for the development of true humanity.

In 1843 Marx said, "Is God sovereign, or is man? One of the two is an untruth, even if an existing untruth."[5] This quote is revealing in that it shows that for Marx atheism is not just the denial of God's existence, but, more importantly, of his *dominion*. People must be free. They must not have a Lord above them. This element of rebellion against the gods, this demand to be his own lord, finds expression in Marx's very earliest writings. For Marx, Prometheus, with his rebellious creed "I hate all gods," is "the most eminent saint and martyr in the philosophical calendar."[6]

It is because of this desire for dominion that Marx rejects the biblical doctrine of creation. Marx sees that if humanity has a Creator, it would also have a Lord.[7] Marx's decision in favor of the theory of the self-origin of the world, seemingly a scientific hypothesis, has its roots in his decision against the kingdom of God. His argument is not free from prejudice or demand. Michael Bakunin, the father of modern political anarchism and Marx's colleague in the beginning of the international labor movement, stated the argument in this form: Men shall be free—hence God must not exist.[8] Thus, the critique of religion begins with a presupposition about humanity and moves to an assertion about God. It is above all the denial of God's rule, and from there it derives its pathos.[9]

"Criticism of religion is the premise of all criticism." One has to grasp the meaning of this statement to understand the pre-eminence of the criticism of religion in Marxist thought. One must see its significance as historical, biographical and motivational. Again and again attempts are made to minimize the atheism in Marxism in order to woo support from Christians. We are told that "Marxism is nothing but an economic system. It has nothing to do with faith. As a Christian one can also be a Marxist." The answer to this must be no. As a Christian one may well be a socialist; that is, one may plead for the common ownership of certain forms of property and production (and of course there have been numerous forms of socialism before, after and at the time of Marx). But one cannot simultaneously be a Marxist and a Christian, for Marxism stands not only for a certain doctrine of property but also for a comprehensive world view to which atheism is an important presupposition.

There are some who contend that atheism and the critique of religion are not essential parts of Marxism. They suggest that these theses are merely accidental elements resulting from the particular conditions of the early historic encounter of Marxism with religion, and that Marxism should and could shed its atheistic components. The reply to this is that it certainly should! But if it did, it would no longer be Marxism. Whoever maintains that atheism is optional to Marxism must either be unfamiliar with the primary sources or guilty of consciously trying to mislead others.

Nobody should underestimate the philosophical consistency of the Marxist system of thought. The abrogation of its atheism would necessarily imply the abolition of its historical materialism and thus its anthropology, its eschatology and its ethics. After such a process of reduction Marxism would just be another form of socialism. That reduction would have completely altered the substance of Marxism. The process could be compared to demanding that Christianity give up its belief in God, the divinity of Christ, the rebirth of man and Jesus' Second Coming, as well as its particular stance on ethics. Christianity could then no doubt qualify as a form of humanism. But it would no longer be Christianity. Of course there have been some who wanted just that kind of change in Christianity. But, I would like to believe, the majority of Christians have always rejected that suggestion as nonsense. And one can expect a similar reaction on the part of Marxists. Just as a Christian could not say that belief in God was a matter of personal taste, no orthodox Marxist would say that atheism was a matter of choice for Marxists. When you are a Marxist, you are necessarily also an atheist.

Marxists themselves tell us, "Ideological coexistence is as impossible as fried snowballs." Marxism and Christianity are basically incompatible. The strong desire of some theologians for accommodation cannot obscure the fact that atheism and the critique of religion are the starting point and the most basic element of the Marxist program. Marxism is dyed-in-the-wool atheism.

"For Germany the criticism of religion is in the main complete, and criticism of religion is the premise of all criticism." We have seen what the second portion of this sentence means. What then does the first portion mean? To what is Marx referring? Who completed the critical task in Germany?

Feuerbach: Theology as Anthropology
Ludwig Feuerbach, born in 1804, was fourteen years older than Marx, and he spent his whole life working on the critique of the Christian religion. Feuerbach is the intellectual father not only of Marx's critique of religion but

also of Sigmund Freud's. Thus, although sometimes ignored, Feuerbach's thought represents one of the most influential philosophical systems of the nineteenth and twentieth centuries.

Feuerbach, who died in 1872, attempted to explain religion, especially the Christian religion, by way of psychology. Faith in God, he thought, owes its existence to the needy, miserable, battered state of the human psyche. In the early stages of development, human beings saw themselves as small and helpless in comparison to the forces of nature which threatened them and which they could not control. In order to avoid despair, people created the myth of a benevolent power behind the universe: God almighty who was to represent superiority over nature.

These ideas are in themselves not new. In substance they already appeared in the works of French atheistic materialists Holbach and Helvetius before the French Revolution. Feuerbach developed them into what we call the *projection theory* of religion. A slide projector enlarges a small slide and projects it onto a wide screen. In a similar fashion, God is seen to be "nothing other than" the image of man and his attributes, enlarged and projected onto heaven. God is the expression of the essence of humanity, stripped of all earthly limitations. That is Feuerbach's basic thesis.[10]

This idea of an explanation for the origin of the concept of God (which, by the way, was already hinted at in Goethe's *Faust*[11]) is present in Feuerbach's very earliest writings, around 1830. There is a series of poems in which Feuerbach mocks believers, especially the Pietists with whom he feels positively disgusted.[12] Then he declares that in religion man makes himself an object apart from himself.[13] Humanity contemplates its own nature in God, whom it imagines to be another, alien being. Religion is the *self-alienation* of humanity.

Later Feuerbach sought to explain the genesis of the concept of God along the lines of the two paths of medieval

speculation about God. One path followed the enlarge-
ment of human attributes, the other the negation of them.
In the first, one arrives at the notion of God by expanding
on human qualities: humans have limited knowledge, God
is omniscient; humans have limited strength, God is almighty, and so on. The other way of discovering the attributes of God was by negation. God is the wholly other; he
is not like humanity: humanity is dependent, God is independent; humanity is finite, God is infinite; humanity is
material, God is immaterial, immortal and so on. The
image of God, therefore, may be produced either by intensifying the human attributes or by asserting the antithesis
of them.[14]

In his famed primary work *The Essence of Christianity*
(1841), Feuerbach tried to consistently reduce divine attributes to human qualities. He applies this method to all the
various divisions of Christian doctrine one by one. God as
Love and as Person, the Trinity, the doctrines of creation
and providence, the divinity of Christ and his Incarnation,
virgin birth and resurrection from the dead—everything is
reduced to basic human conditions. For example, Feuerbach asserts that the doctrine of the Trinity is based on
the belief that God does not live alone, but in communion
(of the three persons of the Godhead). This, the critic says,
is nothing but the religious (that is, alienated) way of saying that togetherness is one of the highest human values.[15]
Methodologically speaking, the theological sentence *God
is living-in-community* is turned into the anthropological
statement *Living in community is godly*, that is, of ultimate concern to humanity.

Briefly, this critique of religion, as it is applied to religious pronouncements, consists of the reversal of the
biblical idea that "God created man in his own image"
(Gen. 1:27). Feuerbach replies that the central idea is that
man created God in *his* image. The only thing certain in the
statement is *man*.[16] Theology needs to be reduced to
anthropology.

Marx and Feuerbach: Religion as Narcotic

The projection theory and the reversal of religious pronouncements seemed to many to be a plausible method of criticism. It met with immediate approval among the radical youth prior to the revolution of 1848. Frederick Engels wrote concerning Feuerbach's *The Essence of Christianity:* "Enthusiasm was general; we all became at once Feuerbachians."[17] The book's popularity was due to the fact that Feuerbach did not simply assert that "humanism is right and religion is wrong; man is the highest being, not God." Instead, he reduced religion *itself* to humanism in a most ingenious way by saying that people venerate their own nature as an alien being. In giving all honor to God, humanity deprives itself of it.

Karl Marx, too, strongly praised Feuerbach's theory of religion and adopted it.[18] He called it the one real revolution and renovation in recent philosophy. Against this backdrop of Feuerbach's theory of religion, one can understand Marx's statement that "the more man puts into God, the less he retains in himself." It means that humanity will not be able to develop and improve until it has abolished the idea of God. The concept of God here takes on the look of a *vampire* which sucks out real human life. From this view it follows that human progress will be possible only when man is finished with religion.[19]

Feuerbach's criticism of religion, by the way, is also in detail the immediate reference point for Marx's essay of 1844. Marx says that man created in religion a fantasy picture of the way life *should* be because he found the actual conditions of life so unjust. This statement assumes Feuerbach's theory that the idea of God originates as the antithesis to man's present predicament,[20] although one feels already that whereas Feuerbach looked at the human predicament as regards nature, Marx thinks of social oppression.

One of Marx's most famous dictums, religion "is the *opium* of the people"[21] can also be understood in the light of this critique of religion. Marx saw religion as the consolation of humanity—a dream and design for true humanity in heaven, while on earth there is only inhumanity. Later this was restyled into "religion is opium *for* the people," which focuses on the ruling class which employs religion as a means to divert the attention of the masses from their miserable condition.

Karl Marx did not invent this comparison of religion with opium. *Opium* used in a figurative sense was current in the literature of Heinrich Heine, Marx's poet friend, in his years of exile in Paris. This same comparison occurs in a review by the German poet laureate Goethe of a volume of sermons by F. A. Krummacher, one of the best-known German evangelicals of the nineteenth century. He was a pastor in Wuppertal, which, as one of the first German cities to develop the textile industry, was also one of the first to experience the atrocities of early capitalism. So Goethe describes these sermons as *narcotics* for those poor people, who otherwise would have nothing to look forward to in their daily labors and drudgery. Certain types of religion are calculated to work like opium, drugging, numbing and removing people to a world of fantasy where they can forget the inhuman conditions of their lives.[22]

In the context of Marx's essay of 1844, the concept of religion as opium underlines once again the weight of the statement, "Criticism of religion is the premise of all criticism." It is the noetic prerequisite. Before one can begin to change the world, one must first do away with opium and begin to see things clearly. As Marx says, the destruction of religion is necessary, so that man will discard his illusions and regain his senses, stop revolving around God as his illusory sun and begin to "revolve round himself and therefore round his true sun."[23]

Marx Moves beyond Feuerbach:
The New Quest for History
In principle, Marx adopted Feuerbach's method which is

the reduction of theological statements to anthropological ones. Yet he went on to raise three criticisms of his own against Feuerbach.

First, as opposed to Feuerbach, Marx demands practice. Feuerbach never got past the realm of theory, but Marx asserts that a truth must not only be recognized, but also realized in practical life. This is why Marx formulates his famous Thesis XI concerning Feuerbach (1845), which we quoted earlier: "Philosophers have only *interpreted* the world in different ways; the point is to *change* it." Marx demands change, not just meditation on and interpretation of the world. New insights must not remain insights; they must be used to reshape the world politically and economically in every respect. Based on this, from the theoretical criticism of religion there will follow atheist conduct and lifestyle.[24]

Second, Marx postulates a concrete sociological approach to religion. Feuerbach described man as the root soil of religion, but Marx went further. He asked: What is man? Is he merely a theoretical concept, a thought, as God was before? Marx answers no. He writes in 1844, "But *man* is no abstract being squatting outside the world. Man is *the world of man*, state, society."[25] This means that the political and social conditions in the world truly represent real human life and determine human production. Concerning the criticism of religion, Feuerbach's theoretical, abstract, psychological critique has to be replaced with a practical, concrete, sociological critique of religion.

Third, Marx asserts that reality is always tied to time. Feuerbach's psychological critique of religion was taken to refer to *all* times or *any* time, and thus ended up being far too general. And even if Feuerbach's explanation of religion were taken to apply only to prehistoric time (that is, the earliest members of the human race), it was much too inexact to be able to so illuminate people about the genesis of religion as to overcome it.[26] Rather, every single religion or religious impulse must at every moment be explicable—

in an atheist manner. Only when we are able to explain plausibly the origins of and reasons for Christianity or any other particular religion will the critique of religion be complete.

Marx goes beyond Feuerbach in that he postulates the *historical* critique of religion. He made an attempt at this himself in a speech before the German Workers' Association in London in 1847. He supported the theory of G. F. Daumer, who held that Christianity was merely the further development of the Phoenician cult of Moloch (which we know from the Old Testament). The Phoenicians, or Philistines, used to sacrifice their first-born. This practice was prohibited in Israel as reported in Deuteronomy 18:10, "There shall not be found among you any one who burns his son or his daughter." Marx, however, links the Phoenician practice with the allegations made by some ancient critics that in the early church children were sacrificed in celebration of the Eucharist ("sacrificing the Son to the Father"). In Protestantism, Marx continues, one would now only find spiritualized forms of that ancient practice, therefore there were many more imbeciles in Protestantism. According to Marx, Daumer's critique had given Christianity the final push, and the edifice of fraud and prejudice was now collapsing.[27]

Unfortunately for Marx, his principal witness in the case against Christianity, Daumer, soon converted to Roman Catholicism and publicly revoked his theories. (His theories had not actually been taken very seriously by scholars.) With this, Marx's attempt at the historical annihilation of Christianity proved futile.

Since that time Marxists have continually tried to complete this task and must necessarily do so. A materialistic philosophy of history—Marxism poses as historical materialism—must produce some explanation of the Christian faith from socio-economic causes. The Marxist program demands an explanation for the genesis of Christianity. It must be explained as a particular stage in the development of material production and its social context.[28]

Frederick Engels in his old age subscribed to the hypothesis that Christianity must have arisen from the religious ferment and social misery of the ancient Near East sometime in the second century A.D. Christ is seen as the ideal image of a comforter and Savior, a spiritual product of the economic misery of the lower classes of Mediterranean society in the second century. There was no historical Jesus. He was the popular symbol of a religious idea which may be traced back to stoicism and Hellenistic Judaism, especially Philo.[29]

That is the most prominent explanation of Christianity which Marxism thus far has achieved. Are Marx and Engels right? Is religion simply the invention of the human imagination? What are we to make of the Marxist critique?

Chapter 4

The Legitimacy and Limit of the Marxist Critique

We cannot simply dismiss Marx's critique of religion. Some of his points may indeed be legitimate. We must find the truth where we can. We must separate the valid criticisms from the invalid ones so that we can learn from our mistakes. Then we may go on to point out where Marx is in error.

Theology: Much Ado about Ourselves

The legitimacy of Feuerbach's and Marx's criticism is to be found in its unearthing of a secret anthropocentrism in large areas of theology and religion. They are correct in saying that some facets of religion, including aspects of the history of Christianity, have merely human origins. For example, Feuerbach wrote a special treatise on "The Nature of Faith in the Writings of Luther." He collected an astonishing number of quotations which seem to give religious man a powerful role in faith, thus lending credence to the assertion that God is but a product of the human imagination.[1]

Feuerbach's own generation of theologians furnished him with a great deal of brilliant evidence for his hypothesis. Friedrich Schleiermacher, often called the church father of the nineteenth century, described the "feeling of unconditioned dependence" as the basis of our consciousness of God.[2] He believed it was possible to recite the whole contents of theology without making use of the concept of God.[3] On the conservative side, his eminent colleague and pupil, August Neander, in turn had a strong influence on the evangelicalism of the first half of the nineteenth century. Neander practically asserted that the richness of feelings make the true theologian ("Pectus est quod facit theologum") and not God's revelation and vocation.[4] Another leading conservative theologian went so far as to say, "I the Christian am, for me the theologian, the particular subject-matter of my science."[5] Again and again, man, humanity, is seen as the central theme of theology and religion. Can we say, then, that Feuerbach was wrong when he said he wished to do nothing but take those theologians seriously in what they said?

We find similar theological trends in the twentieth century. Bultmann in his famous essay "What does it mean to speak about God," wrote that to speak about God is to speak about man.[6] This principle then became the key for his whole program of demythologization. But is this not an immediate parallel to Feuerbach's reduction of theology into anthropology, except for its label?[7]

The God concept of Bultmann's most radical pupil, Herbert Braun of the University of Mainz, would have pleased Feuerbach. Braun clearly links up with Schleiermacher's system as the shrewdest method of doing theology under the conditions of the Enlightenment. He describes God as "the Wherefrom of my being held and being challenged." Here again God is being reduced to a predicate of human experience, rather than a person or an independent entity.[8]

This positing of humanity as the central focus of theology is not a characteristic peculiar to liberal theology. I recently had the opportunity to attend a seminar on the doctrine of God at a theological school which traditionally takes quite a different stand. The professor, with regard to each specification of the traditional doctrine of God, raised the pertinent question of its *actuality* today. In answering this question, the professor reinterpreted various traditional attributes of God in terms of human experiences and aspirations. The doctrine of the Trinity, for instance, he interpreted as suggesting the need for and possibility of solidarity among all human beings. I was surprised. Immanuel Kant, the great initiator of German idealism, had found the Trinity impossible to devour when he tried to reinterpret Christian dogmatics as ethics. The doctrine of the Trinity, he felt, did not yield anything practical for life. Feuerbach, on the other hand, understood exactly how to interpret this doctrine in anthropological terms. He took it to express in mythologized form the value of human fellowship. Of course, the professor in the seminar would never think of reducing theology to anthropology. But by reducing the *actuality* of the doctrine to its anthropological analogy, he ended up with a man-centered approach to theology similar to that of his liberal colleagues. Even if his presuppositions were very different from theologians of the Bultmann school, his results corresponded to the same principle, that is, "to talk about God is to talk about man."

This same reduction of theology to anthropology apparently also lies at the base of the thinking of another professor published recently. A supposedly Lutheran professor of ethics, he interpreted the Ten Commandments as a product of the sacred social history of Israel. The commandment "Thou shalt not commit adultery," for example, was to be seen as a reaction to certain needs felt by the ruling priests, who thereby defended some vested interests. Using categories of religious sociology or psychology to interpret theology is a frequent practice nowadays. This, however, would mean, for instance, that the works of Walther Eichrodt and Gerhard von Rad, which represent efforts to describe a distinct theology of the Old Testament, are merely an intermezzo in the recent history of theological interpretation. We would have to return to seeing the Old (and of course the New) Testament as a collection of documents from the history of religion—a history of human creations and nothing more.

This habit of seeing humanity as the focus of religion is not limited to theological schools. It also determines much of corporate and personal piety among Christians. It is distressing to discover that the history of Christianity is indeed, to a large extent, a history of men and women shaping their own lives of faith. We do not let God be God. In theology we often develop doctrine, for example, the doctrine of God, without asking for his (God's own) doctrine of God; we formulate our theologies without asking for revelation and education by the Spirit of God himself, even though we know that "no one comprehends the thoughts of God except the Spirit of God" (1 Cor. 2:11). Again, in our everyday lives as Christians too often we manifest only human values. God's presence in our lives is like a painted plaster image which is not supposed to speak or to instruct us on what we must do. Our life and faith thus become nothing but a human creation, a piece of human religious history.

Therefore, we should be warned by Feuerbach's and Marx's criticisms of religion. We should change our ways, cease to espouse human designs in religious disguise, and go back to the lordship of God in theory and practice.

Of course, as human witnesses of God we shall always be in danger of letting our talk of God degenerate into our own religious products, indeed, into talk about nothing else than ourselves. This will always happen when we are no longer willing to receive and hear what God has to say, when we suppose we know everything already, and when we demand to reign and not to serve. But the concept of God as a human product, the supremacy of man in theology and religion, will always and inevitably be uncovered and destroyed by Marxist criticism of religion.

Those who make humanity the sole object of theology, who preach and proclaim their own sovereignty instead of God's, who glorify their own religious experiences (a subject dear to evangelicals!) instead of "the mighty works of God" (Acts 2:11), who reduce theology to human existence and endeavor, prepare Christianity for annihilation by the Marxist critique of religion. A theology and piety which secretly glorify humanity—be it credulous, pious humanity or enlightened, unpious humanity—as the center of religion, will soon fall victim to that critical guillotine designed by Feuerbach and kept in working condition by Marxism.

The intellectual presence of this threat should help us all toward self-criticism and toward the dethronement of human reason and sentiment as the sovereign ruler over faith, thinking and action in Christendom. This is necessary at any rate if we are to realize the kingdom of God in God's own world, primarily in theology and the church.

Bringing Back History
During the last few years, Feuerbach's writings have been reprinted in a considerable number of editions, and his ideas are spreading again. His books contain a whole arsenal of arguments against religion. In particular, the psychological critique of religion appears very impressive. I remember an episode which I went through while in the Reading Room of the British Museum in London. I was studying Feuerbach's *The Essence of Christianity*, in which he reduced the various doctrines to mere anthro-

pology one by one. Suddenly the thought hit me, What if he were right? I was horrified. Everything was so colossally plausible, I thought, until I began to observe that Feuerbach throughout evaded every historical question. His critical theory remains timeless. He silently presupposes that Christ never lived, that he was not a figure of history. It is this evasion of historical questions which caused Marx to attempt to improve on Feuerbach's method.

Feuerbach's critical theory nevertheless represents a devastating attack on any nonhistorical conception of Christianity because it puts it under "ideology-suspicion," under the suspicion of being mere theory.

At this point we cannot be content with general statements. Two systems of theology which did not give much consideration to the historicity of the Gospels have been dominant in this century. The theologies of Rudolf Bultmann and Karl Barth (certainly the early Barth) are examples of influential systems of thought which tend to ignore historical questions in Christian doctrine. Both separated the story of the salvation events from objective history in time and space and laid all emphasis on the former: God does not act visibly in history but always remains beyond this world.[9] Where the historical components are thus neglected, Christianity is changed into a system of timeless theological statements. Such a system may take the floor as subjectivism (with which we have already dealt), but also as orthodox objectivism. As opposed to subjectivism, the objectivity of the contents of faith indeed is important and must be maintained. Nevertheless, statements that come with objectivist pathos may yet be only the assertions of a believer, and therefore quite arbitrary, possessing no links to provable reality. Such statements will not be convincing to others when they are cast into question by the critique of religion. Therefore, a theology of objectivity with no emphasis on history is not safe either from the breaking waves of critique.

The study of Feuerbach has taught me that Bultmann's theology can be of no avail for us. One cannot be a Bultmannian in the long run if one wants to withstand the Marxist critique. The emergence of the theology of Bultmann in the twentieth century can be understood only if one assumes that those who adopted this theology had no knowledge of Marxism and its critique of religion. The long-lived influence of Bultmann's theology must be seen as an unhappy development. It is the worst possible preparation of Christian theology for the encounter with the Feuerbach-Marx methodology of criticism, because Bultmann basically reiterates the position of Schleiermacher which Feuerbach found to be such an easy target.

Judgment on the early theology of Karl Barth would not be much different. Barth's theology fights subjectivism by taking refuge in objective statements about the transcendence of God. Barth even praised Feuerbach's critique of religion as one of the most welcome events of the nineteenth century because he felt Feuerbach was an ally at smoking out subjectivism.[10] But Barth's theology sidesteps the issue of the historicity of Christ, denying that it constitutes the primary objectivity of faith and implying that it is of no consequence for faith.[11] In doing this, the early Barth made of theology an arbitrary, dogmatic contention instead of opening the way for others to comprehend God's work in history.

Criticizing Individualism

Not only the subjectivism of much of theology, but also the individualism of religious life becomes subject to the criticism of Marx and Feuerbach. In his very first study of religious criticism, on the religious philosophy of Plutarch, the Hellenistic writer, Marx pointed to the dominant position of individualism in religion. Religion seems to be primarily concerned with the eternal happiness of the individual. As such, religion becomes an addiction to personal spiritual pleasure-seeking.[12]

Marx could not fail to encounter individualism in the modes of expression of Christian piety in the nineteenth century. In hymnals, the "we" of Reformation days had mostly been replaced by the "I" as subject of the hymn. In addition there was the playfulness of expression in the later eighteenth century which tended to reduce the whole world of God and humanity to "I and my sweet Savior." Other tendencies toward individualism resulted from the literary romantic movement which strongly influenced German pietism in the early nineteenth century. This is evidenced in the well-known hymn line of Novalis's, "If only I have him ... I quietly let others walk the wide, bright road." We can be thankful that Feuerbach and Marx subjected the unwarranted individualistic tendencies of theology and piety to a merciless critique.

At the same time, it has to be asked if Marxism is right in saying that Christianity isolates people and destroys natural interpersonal relationships.[13] Certainly people are not being swept as a group into the kingdom of God. God's calling is directed toward individuals: "Rejoice that your names are written in heaven" (Lk. 10:20). The second person singular is appropriate for the present when we are talking about calling and justification. It seems true, then, that the gospel deals with individuals to begin with, in order that each unique person can be accepted by God. "Truly, truly, I say to you, unless one is born anew, he cannot see the kingdom of God" (Jn. 3:3). But it is equally true that from conversion each person is led to and related to other believers and to all neighbors.

Feuerbach always maintained that because Christianity stresses transcendence and the love of God, it could never successfully defend the command to love one's neighbor. He said that if you are looking up to heaven, you cannot at the same time look at your neighbor, unless you are cross-eyed![14] The result is that faith in God and love of neighbor are mutually exclusive. In this way the critic tries to wrestle the command for loving neighbors away from Christianity and claim it for atheistic humanism. According to Feuerbach's logic there can be no care for our neighbor in this world when we believe in the world to come.[15] This is a theme repeated in contemporary times in many forms, including in the "atheistic Christianity" of Dorothee Soelle and others, which asserts that faith must be detrimental to love.[16]

Is it true that faith and love of neighbor are mutually exclusive? Adolf Schlatter, one of the two or three most eminent theologians of our century, always reminded scholars of the need for perception before thinking or theorizing.[17] With regard to our present question, this means that we must observe what is the case before we can draw our conclusions. Love of neighbor and charitable activities are historically the creation of the Judeo-Christian tradition rather than Greek or Renaissance humanism. It therefore seems an impossible enterprise to prove that Christianity, presented as the principle of individual happiness, can have nothing to do with love of neighbor, when in fact historically it has been the source of neighborly love.

When I was studying Greek, I had to translate a piece of papyrus unearthed in the sands of the Nile. In it a migrant worker from Alexandria wrote a letter to his wife in Oxyrynchus, Upper Egypt, saying: "If thou art delivered, if it was a male child, let it (live), if it was female, cast it out."[18] At the same time one could read in the letters of the early church: "Thou shalt not slay the child by procuring abortion; nor, again, shalt thou destroy it after it is born. Thou shalt not withdraw thy hand from thy son, or from thy daughter, but from their infancy thou shalt teach them the fear of the Lord."[19] The old world was uncertain concerning its respect for the life of even a child. The concept of the sanctity of life has come into our civilization through Judaism and Christianity. And what needed to be said in the second century concerning the preservation of the life of the unborn has to be said afresh today.

And again it is Christians, for the most part, who are saying it, not atheists.

This same value has shaped the Christian attitude
toward the sick. Malcolm Muggeridge, one of the wittiest
entertainers of our time who became a Christian some
years ago, was involved in a discussion on TV with a
militant atheist. When attacked with the same argument,
that faith made love impossible, with a twinkle in his
eyes he told this story: "I have recently traveled in Africa,
but I have yet to discover the leper station founded by the
British Humanist Association. The existing stations are
all run by Christians. And the more 'narrow-minded' they
are, the more stations they usually run!"

The result is that while logic may indicate that love for
God excludes love for people, reality tells us something
else. In the history of Christianity, a determined commitment to God has always been the most dependable motivation for service to others.

We must, however, also ask whether or not we have,
in fact, in the practice of our Christianity, opted for
individualism. How far do we "hide . . . from [our] . . .
own flesh" (Is. 58:7), sometimes giving religious reasons?
Do we use transcendence as a pretext to withdraw from
our neighbor's plight? God told his people even in exile
to "seek the welfare of the city where I have sent you into
exile, and pray to the LORD on its behalf" (Jer. 29:7).

Jesus made his disciples a family. Even on the cross he
said to one disciple, "Behold, your mother," and to his
mother he said, "Behold, your son" (Jn. 19:27, 26). He so
constituted the circle of his friends that all who lived
with him and learned from him would never again do
anything on their own. They would know that they
complement each other and must work together. In Jesus
the disciples found an example of caring for all the needy,
including those outside of the church. The question, however, remains: Have we learned and accepted this lesson
from Jesus, or do our lives prove the Marxist criticism of

religion which says that Christianity destroys human relationships and produces indifference toward other people? Could it be that Marx and Feuᵣ ᵣbach were wrong regarding the Initiator of Christianity, but right regarding many of its self-styled followers?

Evaluating Christian Practice

Marx cannot fail to address to Christians the question he raised in respect to Feuerbach: How much is religion, even Christianity, mere theory and contemplation rather than a leading on to action? How much is it an ideological front, a tool of the ruling class, a camouflage of exploitation, a cloud of dust thrown into the eyes of the suppressed, an opiate for the people to anesthetize the miserable masses?

Properly understood, this question is not directed only at members of the ruling class who may try to facilitate their own unholy purposes by recommending the gospel to others. This question is a test for all Christians: How much is our faith really just a piece of decoration, a prop on the theater of life, a conscious or unconscious maneuver to deceive the people around us? Marxism, in its quest for what is practical and concrete, for us means the inquiry into the reality and seriousness of our Christian discipleship. Engels used to quote the proverb he learned from British workers: "The proof of the pudding is in the eating."[20] In other words, you will know the quality of the pudding only as you try it; practical application determines the value of a system, not contemplation.

How far are theory and practice in consonance in our lives? Is God an unreality when it comes to action? Is he a myth, a phantom? Is he the product of a magnificently fertile imagination, a picture without life, arrogantly placed by human hands into the heaven of man's religious empire? Christianity is surprisingly often seen as merely a means of observation and critical examination of the world. Can we claim that Christians, as they live today, represent the biblical faith?

Surely Marxism itself will one day finally fail the test of practice. Nevertheless, the call for practice represents a valid criticism, one which we ought to have been aware of all along: "If any man's will is to do his [God's] will, he shall know whether the teaching is from God or whether I am speaking on my own authority" (Jn. 7:17).

We can benefit greatly by a critique from Marxism which uncovers our failures and omissions and reminds us of the norms of the New Testament. In the encounter with Marxism we are being reminded of our innermost commitment. Marxism becomes a challenge to Christians to *live* our faith—a faith embodied in our actions.

Limits to the Marxist Critique

After discussing the validity of the Marxist criticism of religion it remains to examine its limitations. Next to its good sense we must also perceive its nonsense.

We have seen how Marx, pinning down the inadequacies of Feuerbach's method, demanded its improvement in the direction of a historical critique. We have also seen how he and later Engels tried to fulfill this demand by criticizing religion from a historical standpoint. In so doing, however, Marx made his position untenable at a number of points.

If Christianity is to have originated outside Palestine in the second century, then the New Testament books must be dated much later than tradition has so far led us to believe. This is what Engels assumed in his essay of 1883, "The Book of Revelation." Along with the more radical group of nineteenth-century theologians, Engels believed Revelation to be the earliest book of the New Testament, originating with a Jewish sect. This seed blossomed into Christianity, which was officially received by the emperors of the fourth century. In Revelation, Engels saw the figure of a heavenly, mythic, ideal Christ—a Savior who in the Gospels written later was turned into a historical person.[21] Thus the foundations of Christianity were turned upside-down by giving them a second-century date which would preclude their historicity.

Many objections could be raised to this conjecture about the dates of the New Testament books. But the most devastating is that in the beginning of the twentieth century, a piece of papyrus containing part of the Gospel of John was found in Egypt. It was given a date by archaeologists on the basis of outward appearance of sometime in the early second century. Consequently, it is assumed that the Gospel of John (supposedly the last one of the four Gospels to be written) must have existed in written form by at least the year 90 or 95. Now, if Revelation was written in A.D. 68 or 69, a date also accepted by Engels, there would not be enough time for that sectarian Jewish myth to develop into the full-blown picture of Christ which is presented in the Gospel of John. That the papyrus found contains John 18: 31-33 and 37-38, a section which does not give timeless discourses but speaks of the historical person of Pilate and Jesus' interrogation, creates another difficulty for a non-historical interpretation. "Further discoveries in Egypt," which Engels had hoped would support his cause, have instead done much to chasten critical theories. It seems, in fact, that they have destroyed the hypothesis that Christianity owes its origin to certain economic conditions in the second century.

As to the *place* of the origin of Christianity Engels was not so sure of himself. At one point he was certain that Christianity must have come into existence in Egypt.[22] In another essay he grants that it may have originated in Palestine.[23] In a third place, he admits that he does not have the answer, not even a historical-materialistic answer, and he writes: "The new world religion, Christianity, had already quietly come into being."[24] He simply presupposes what he had previously tried to explain.

In a similar fashion, Lenin began with the contention that Christ had never lived. He sought to support his opinion with one of the most eccentric books of the debate on the life of Jesus, *Die Christusmythe* by Arthur Drews.[25] The following statements by Albert Schweitzer apply to Drews as well as to Marxists who seek to deny the historicity of Christ:

> *The temptation to deny the historicity of Jesus stems from the lack of ancient, primary information about him in the Greco-Roman profane literature.... If one does not wish to accept that contemporary secular historiography did not mention Jesus because it did not pay any attention to his appearance, one may feel entitled to, instead of tracing Christianity back to Jesus Christ, explain him as the creation of a religious movement which for some reason tried to legitimate itself historically in this way. The most obvious solution in this case is to let such a movement originate during a time of religious ferment, such as existed in the Greco-Roman world in the first and second centuries of our chronology.*
>
> *One may, though, ... also conceive of Jesus—as Arthur Drews did in his Christusmythe (1909)—as a figure of mythical origin which later assumed historical features. Archetypes of the dying and rising Christ could then be dying and resurrected godheads of Greek-Oriental myths like Tammuz, Attis, Adonis and Osiris. Should one, however, against all expectation, not really succeed in explaining the rise of a Christ myth from this material, then there are astral myths still available. On one of those Drews fell back in the second edition of his work (1911). Christ crucified is Orion having become a God-man, who with arms spread, hangs on the World Tree of the Milky Way surrounded by the signs of the zodiac like a gang of villains. Yet if the theory of the nonhistoricity of Jesus is intended to proceed somewhat scientifically it must not only explain the genesis of his mythical personality, which already is rather difficult, but also make plausible how this invented, non-Jewish personality happened to appear in Judaism at the time*

of the first emperors. That is a hopeless enterprise. ...
The present and future challenges of the historical exis-
tence of Jesus will find things yet more difficult than the
earlier ones. [26]
Earlier theorists could claim that historical research had
not yet reached dependable conclusions. But today it is
nearly impossible to deny the historicity of Jesus. The attempt at a socio-historical explanation of the genesis of
Christianity has failed again. The criticism of religion,
then, especially in the sense put forward by historical
materialism, is not "in the main complete." Rather, up till
now it has failed.

The failure of this kind of historical critique of Christianity is due to the intrinsic timelessness and lack of historical understanding of Feuerbach's theory of religion
Marx's attempt to introduce the historical element into
the theory was bound to run into difficulties. Feuerbach's
formula is unfit to contain history. In fact, he arrived at it
by eliminating history. The theory works only on the sort
of timeless statements which are typical of religious
philosophy.

Right at the outset Feuerbach turned the biblical statements containing action, events and history into proposi-
tions about states of being, as in philosophy of religion.
Then he would submit them to his process of reversal.
Even grammar, as may be easily shown, witnesses to this.
The action-verb sentences are replaced by "is" sentences, with a timeless character; "God created man after
his own image" has to be turned into "Man is the image of
God" before this can be reversed into "God is the image of
man." The same reversal is applied to "God is love." But
it is often forgotten that the biblical statement "God is
love" (1 Jn. 4:16) is identified by its context: "In this is
love, ... that he [God] loved us and sent his Son to be the
expiation for our sins" (1 Jn. 4:10). God's love became action. Feuerbach, though, does not know how to deal with
action and history; thus he never approaches the aspect of

the historical anchorage of the Christian faith.[27]

The lack of historical differentiating in Feuerbach is moreover obvious in that, as far as his critique is concerned, all religions and religious philosophies are the same to him. He apparently first developed his method of religious criticism as a critique of the philosophy of religion and the concept of God as absolute personality as taught in the school of Schelling.[28] But then without further qualification Feuerbach applied the same method to a completely different subject, the historical *events* of the origin of Christianity. With this he demonstrated that from the start he looked at Christianity as a kind of religious philosophy and ignored its historical basis and content.

Marx did not begin much differently. His own first critique of religion dealt with the writings of the pre-Christian philosopher Plutarch. Here Feuerbach's method seems to be very appropriate. But then Marx went on to say that Plutarch is exemplary of the nature of religion and therefore the critique of Plutarch is valid for all religions, Christianity included.[29] Consequently, he never dealt with Christianity in detail, but referred to Feuerbach's *The Essence of Christianity* as having already performed that task. In throwing together Hellenistic religious philosophy and Christianity, Marx also demonstrated both a lack of differentiation in the history of religion and an indifference to the historical basis of Christianity.

The historical element, therefore, has been eliminated wherever Feuerbach's and Marx's method of criticism is applied to Christianity. History, however, is characteristically part and parcel of the Christian faith. If we eliminate the historical element from the Christian message and tradition, the "when Cyrenius was governor of Syria" and "suffered under Pontius Pilate," then we have changed the very nature of the subject before we begin to criticize it. This also explains why, when Feuerbach presents it, Christian doctrine takes on such a strange, alien look. What Feuerbach presents is something quite different from the New Testament message. The real New Testament message is not what is criticized.

This is also indicated by Feuerbach's unwillingness in *The Essence of Christianity* to quote the Gospels to any extent. Instead, he makes use of quotations from obscure medieval authors in order to distill from them the "essence" of Christianity.[30] In Feuerbach's view one religious document seems to be as good as any other, and the precedence of historical origins does not seem to cross his mind.

The revelation of God in Jesus Christ is the invincible rock of faith. Yet the Marxist critique is weakest concerning the person of Jesus. The critics are loud and self-assured when attacking the sins of medieval popes and theologians. They are much more subdued when they deal with Paul's letters to his churches, and mostly silent in view of the person of Jesus of Nazareth.[31] Where the anchor of Christian faith lies deepest in the ocean floor of history, criticism is powerless. Perhaps it is only valid as long as it is uncovering the hidden dominion of man in religion. And that does not apply to Jesus.

The Core of Christianity

What remains? Is there a core of truth left once the deformities of Christian theology and practice have been destroyed by Marxist criticism? Or, in the words of the original thesis, is the criticism of religion in the main complete, or not?

There seem to be two major points at which the Marxist critique of religion breaks down. First, there is the unsolved riddle of the genesis of Christianity: the resurrection of Jesus Christ and the bold beginning of evangelism by his disciples. No one to date has been able to give a conclusive answer to the question of how and why the followers of a preacher who was a "failure" and was executed could, with tremendous confidence, go to all parts of the world to proclaim his resurrection and rule. The New

Testament explanation is that the risen Christ himself sent them, and that he himself gave these uneducated people the necessary gifts and talents. This answer seems more plausible than the many and varied conjectures which have been devised as alternatives. Believing in the Gospel reports is more justifiable than trusting in socio-historical theories which have not stood the test of time. The criticism of religion, especially of historical Christianity, is certainly not "in the main complete." And if it is not, then what about the foundation of Marx's other criticisms, about which he said "criticism of religion is the premise of all criticism"?

Next to the historical roots of the Christian faith, which have not been removed successfully, there remains the perfectly conceivable and yet extraordinary and unforgettable person of Jesus of Nazareth. His challenge remains. It is still true that today Jesus of Nazareth invites men and women to live in fellowship with him and to be changed and directed by him in much the same way as he changed and guided his disciples in the first century.

A spiritual experience which changes people for the better cannot be ignored by any responsible critic of religion, no matter how critically minded. No one who has seen, for example, the destruction brought about by alcohol abuse in a person, a family or a nation can ignore a religion in which men and women are liberated from alcoholism and its ravages. But alcoholics are not the only examples. I have always been impressed by the story of how Jesus healed a demon-possessed man; when people came they "saw the demoniac sitting there, clothed and in his right mind (Mk. 5:15). The betterment of humanity will be a convincing argument for Christianity to those who value their nation's welfare more than any ideological program.

Renewed men and women form the true foundation of a new order. Therefore, the true dialogue between Christians and Marxists centers on the question of the creation of new men and women. That is the decisive point, not the criticism of religion.

For Christians, the consequence of all this must be to renew their commitment to God. He is to be the ruling factor in life instead of the forgotten factor. This should apply in our own lives as well as in the lives of the communities to which we belong. On all accounts we must see to it that God and his commandments are taken account of in all human deliberations so that no one may imagine that God is dead because he is no longer mentioned.

And beyond this, we must show that God is not just a language event. God himself can speak to people through our *lives*. It is our weakness as Christians that too often we have not experienced the reality of God. This, on the one hand, makes us vulnerable to atheist arguments. On the other, it makes us very theoretical. When we speak of the reality of God, we tend to sound as though we are speaking about life on Mars—no one knows much about it and even if one did, it would not make a difference in everyday life. So, more than anything else we need the experience of God's healing presence in our personal and social lives. Experience and deed are the best answers to arguments, and the concrete reality of God is the most effective means to counter atheism. We need to pray: "let us, Lord, experience your reality and make it visible to other people."[32]

Part III

Marxist-Leninist Ethics

Chapter 5

The Ethics of Marx

In studying the classic writings of Marxism-Leninism, Christian readers again and again are fascinated by the apparent structural similarity between Marxist and Christian ethics even when their aims and means are widely different. Our purpose in these next chapters is to compare the ethics of Marx and Lenin's revolutionary ethos with Christian ethics in order to discover their formal analogies.

We are not assuming here that Marxism and Christianity could merge. As we observed before, Marxism and Christianity are incompatible because Marxism—differing in this respect from other forms of socialism—contains an intrinsic atheism. Nevertheless, the ethics of both Christianity and Marxism are at least formally comparable because they both represent programs of establishing a sovereignty: the sovereign in Christianity is God; in Marxism it is man.

An analogy, by comparing two essentially different entities, helps us to better understand both of them. In a similar way, comparing Marxist and Christian ethics may serve to remind ordinary Christian opinion today of the true nature of New Testament ethics.

Are Marxist Ethics Possible?

Werner Sombart, distinguished liberal economist and sociologist at the turn of the century, posed this question and answered it with a straight no. The notion of ethics, that is, of active choice, planned or spontaneous, must be incompatible with the concept of determinism. Under the banner of "historical materialism," Marxism, especially in the nineteenth century emphasized that historical developments take place out of necessity. The revolution, the great future turning point and reversal of all things, was inevitable. Therefore, nothing could be done to hasten it, and nothing could be done to prevent the revolution.[1]

Vernon Venable, the social philosopher, dealt with the question of the possibility of a Marxist ethic in a special monograph. Could an ethical theory be obtained from a system asserting that history consists of inevitable developments? His answer was no. In Marxism, Venable pointed out, one does not think in terms first of consciousness and then of being. One does not begin by educating humanity and then hoping for changes in its material basis, for example, its mode of production. It is always the other way around. The "basis" determines the "superstructure." Being determines consciousness. And, in the same vein, Is determines Ought. The development of the material basis (for example, technology and industrial organization, which Marx called forces of production) would determine the intellectual development of mankind, including moral concepts. Therefore, under the proposition of historical materialism, moral appeals must be senseless. Especially in his later years, Marx had seen people as simply particles in the movement of anonymous processes, bits of animated material which therefore could not be held responsible for their actions. Marx believed the revolution would not have to be initiated by people but would come about with historical necessity. In such a context an ethical imperative was out of place.[2]

Helmut Thielicke has reached similar conclusions in his *Theological Ethics*. Ethics, Thielicke asserts, assumes a basic distinction between subject and object. Each situation necessitating an ethical decision requires a person facing a choice about a person or a thing. In any system of monism, therefore, be it idealistic or materialistic, ethics was as good as impossible because this fundamental distinction between subject and object had been obscured. Indeed, the place of ethics in a system of monistic idealism, such as Hegel's philosophy of mind, would be as uncertain as its place in Marx's monistic materialism.[3]

Martin Buber, the eminent Jewish philosopher of religion, has also examined the possibility of a Marxist ethic. He, too, has come to a negative conclusion. His argumentation is particularly impressive. From the Old Testament, he draws a basic distinction between prophetic and apocalyptic statements. Prophetic proclamations both announced judgment *and* offered an alternative. They called people to make a decision. "Because of and as long as man exists, at any hour, however late, change may yet come about, toward disaster or toward salvation."[4] Apocalyptic statements, on the other hand, are very different. These statements proclaimed a future which is essentially already at hand or is predestined and as such inescapable. Rightly it was called apocalyptic, for the only part which human beings may play in these events is to reveal that which is already settled and established. Real choice and human effort find no room here.

Buber thinks that Marx's statements are of the apocalyptic variety. In some places Marx did express that the

new forces in society needed new men and women to
bring about good. But in light of Marx's theory that people
are determined by the conditions under which they live,
this talk about new men was, to use Buber's own simile, a
scattered spark of prophetic fire.

Determinism vs. Human Action

Martin Buber's analysis seems convincing, especially in
light of the many sages who, throughout the history of
thought, let themselves be pushed into an alternative between determinism and human action. Often, when they
felt they possessed a comprehensive system of knowledge
explaining the cosmos and history, there was little emphasis on ethics. Rather, one embraced a largely con-
templative attitude. This can be seen in representatives of
early Jewish apocalyptic. They saw human activity reduced to waiting for the Day of the Lord and perhaps cal-
culating the events leading up to it. (But this attitude is by
no means confined to early Judaism.)

There are, however, some philosophers and theologians
who believe that determinism and human freedom are,
indeed, compatible. One of the most eminent theologians
of the turn of the century, Wilhelm Herrmann, a prominent Kantian, consciously accepted the idea of determinism and nevertheless wrote an important volume of
ethics.[5] He directs us to consider the fact that in Christian
theology in general God's predestination and the instruction for men and women to live holy lives constantly go
together. In the New Testament the imperative directed at
the believer is often linked to the indicative description of
God's intention and action. Philippians 2:12-13 is a prominent instance of this startling dialectic: "Work out your
own salvation with fear and trembling; for God is at work
in you, both to will and to work for his good pleasure."

One might object that this particular paradox is just the
sort of irrationalism one would expect from theologians,
whereas after what we have heard from Sombart and

others, Marxism, with its claim to rationality, would be expected to be consistent—consistently deterministic. Yet Marx believes in a dialectical approach. In an essay on the subject, Helmut Gollwitzer (theologian at the Free University of West Berlin, who is well acquainted with the problems of Marxism) has pointed out that theories in biology and natural history could never cogently say anything about the actual progress of human history. Again and again unexpected turns are found in the history of individuals and in the history of the world. A simple, mechanistic understanding of materialism as a world view will always encounter insoluble problems not only in ethics but also in eschatology. This would be true of the Marxism of the late nineteenth century. Gollwitzer notes that in the development of Marxism this theoretical dilemma is being cut like the Gordian knot: it *had* to be, simply because people are constantly faced with the need to decide and to act. Their own nature and the nature of their surroundings force them to. And Gollwitzer points out that in the history of Marxism more and more the emphasis is shifting from expounding historical laws to requiring people to work toward the goal envisioned.[6]

Marx's Approach to Ethics

Looking back at Marx's early essay "Contribution to the Critique of Hegel's Philosophy of Law," published in 1844 in the *Deutsch-Französische Jahrbücher*, we see that there was an ethical element present from the beginning. How do ethical appeal and conformity to historical laws relate to each other? The answer is that Marx demands action that corresponds with the historical development which he takes to be necessary and imminent, and which he thinks he can anticipate and define.

The backdrop for Marx's thought was an event in the history of German idealism which at the same time signaled the end of that idealism. This was the discovery of *man* as the primary theme of philosophy. The new phi-

losophy no longer attempted to know about the being or
history of God. Nor did it seek to expound a phenome-
nology of mind. It demanded the abandonment of all metaphysics and reduced not only theology, but also philosophy to anthropology. Thus, with the help of Feuerbach,
philosophy turned a corner, and the effects of this change
are still felt today. In the judgment of Karl Marx, Feuerbach's writings were the only recent ones which contained a real theoretical revolution. [7]

Feuerbach's revolution was, however, only theoretical.
As we have already seen in his criticism of religion, after
1843 Marx began to move beyond Feuerbach in order to re-
establish a relevance to history and practice, which Marx
thought Feuerbach had lost. In contrast to the undia-
lectical philosophy of Feuerbach, Marx tried to reintro-
duce Hegel's dialectic of mind as a process in reality. With
regard to anthropology, this meant that man is not (as with
Feuerbach) an abstract, timeless entity ("the essence of
man") but a *being in becoming*. [8] Consequently, Marx came
to speak not so much of anthropology or of the nature of
man, but of an anthropogenesis of man, a history of development of his nature. The aim of a historical process,
an aim which is still to be attained, is to develop true
human nature. Marx's concept of man is historical.

So Marx does not have in mind—or at least he says he
hasn't—an ideal theory about human nature with which to
approach reality and on which to base an ethical theory.
Rather, he intends to read from the existing "untrue"
being of man his true being, from the existing inhumanity
of man his true humanity. It seems, however, that anyone
who is dissatisfied with the present state of affairs must
have in mind an idea or a material expectation, a pre-
sentiment of what that state which would satisfy him
would look like. Marx must have then presupposed some
"idea of the just" (Dahrendorf), [9] some ethical standard
with which to approach the present evil. His humanistic
concept of justice surfaces in many places in the exchange

of letters between Feuerbach, Ruge and himself, which he published in 1844 along with his essay on Hegel's philosophy of law.

The element of ethics is quite apparent when Marx, leaving Feuerbach behind, calls for the realization of that which has been recognized theoretically—when he calls for practice. Even where Marx contends that the *ought* is to be derived from the *is*, truth approaches existing conditions again as an *ought*. The aim of truth is to expose the true being of man. Marx's language betrays his belief in ethics when he describes the task at hand and emphasizes what must be done. He says: "The *task* of history is . . . to establish the *truth of this world*. . . . The immediate *task* of philosophy . . . is to unmask self-estrangement."[10] The continuing and present task of philosophy is theoretical—exposing the reality which is not yet consonant with its own deepest truth. History, on the other hand, is given the practical task of bringing the known truth to power—or does Marx even think of "History gives the task . . . ?" His own text, "The task of history . . . " is ambivalent.

Later Marx not only speaks of a task, but characterizes it as a *must*: "The actual pressure must be made more pressing by adding to it consciousness of pressure . . . these petrified relations must be forced to dance by singing their own tune to them!"[11] That is the task of consciousness raising, of agitation, of propaganda. Practical action is also being encouraged when Marx later concludes: "The criticism of religion ends with the teaching that *man is the highest being for man*, hence with the *categorical imperative to overthrow all relations* in which man is a debased, enslaved, forsaken, dispicable being."[12] Here we even find the central concept of ethics—an imperative, moreover, a categorical one! What is peculiar, however, is that Marx's pleas for action are usually addressed to an obscure subject. They are aimed at "history," "philosophy," the vague entity "one" or given to anonymous subjects. Nevertheless, it is of course people, groups of people, who are being challenged to take action. Men and women must be the carriers of that historical development which Marx described as the subject of action. Human history has taken on the attributes of Hegel's "Weltgeist" (World Mind), that concept of a deity which developed itself to perfection through history.

From these considerations we may draw a couple of conclusions: First, Marx subjects all demanded action to a certain *aim* or purpose, which is to make people human again, to make man really the "highest" being in the world, which, for Marx, he is in truth and in essence. The aim of action is the emancipation of humanity until its nature is fully realized. Above all the various individual demands stands this one "categorical imperative," the one single principle of action and a commission directing all the other instructions.

Second, this principle of action, which was derived from historical development, is then applied again to the different situations and conditions of historical development. This situational application and determination pointed out by the term *immediate* (the "immediate task" of philosophy) is highly significant. Marx's principle of humanizing humanity must be spelled out in concrete, specific tasks when applied to existing conditions. In the printed exchange of letters of 1843, Marx argues at great length for the need to continually set out from ongoing political developments instead of simply proclaiming abstract programs. The aim of emancipation is never pursued independent of an analysis of the given situation.[13] But likewise all situations are regulated by the overall aim. Purpose and situation are therefore the two basic categories of revolutionary action which our analysis will have to pursue further.

Chapter 6

The Ethics of Lenin

Unlike Marx, Lenin said little about the fundamental anthropological meaning of revolution (the regeneration of the true nature of man). He said much more about how the revolution is to be brought about. Within this framework we find a large, though not systematically presented, number of pronouncements on ethics. But we would anyway not expect to receive a philosophical treatise from someone who is an international organizer of revolution and a prime minister.

The connection with the Russian revolutionary tradition was decisive for Lenin right from the beginning. When Lenin was seventeen, his much-revered older brother was hanged for his part in an abortive attempt to assassinate the tsar. This was the event which pushed Wladimir Lenin toward revolutionary thinking. He was at

home in the world of revolutionary thought before he became a Marxist. So when he adopted Marxist thought, he
put the emphasis on realization of the revolution, rather
than on waiting for it to come about through some historical law. Therefore, Lenin's stance has also been called
"voluntarism."[1]

In her memoirs Krupskaya, Lenin's life companion, reports how immediately after his arrival in St. Petersburg,
Lenin, then a young attorney by education, comes into
conflict with the Marxists already there. He contemp-
tuously calls them "mechanists," because in his judgment
they conceive of societal processes only in a mechanistic
way. Lenin asserts that such a concept of history would
completely deny the active role of the masses, the proletariat.[2] According to Lenin, one must will the revolution and act to bring it about.

The "Ethics" of Revolution

Lenin seems to present us with two very different approaches to ethics. In the years prior to the revolution of
1917, he formulates instructions for revolutionary action,
elements of an "ethic" of revolution. Concerning these,
the term "ethic" can really be used only in a very general and imprecise sense. For ethics means parallel to
ethos, its Greek root term (originally connoting custom,
the same as the Latin mos, the root term of morality)—the
doctrine of regular moral behavior. To be exact concerning
Lenin we ought to use not ethics but a more neutral term
such as "action theory" and thus speak of Lenin's revolutionary action theory.

Revolution means action creating change, action which
does not take place within the boundaries of traditional
rules and cannot be determined by static norms and timeless laws. Revolutionary action is not subject to any man-
dates specifying the road it is to take. The revolution is
self-determining and self-limiting. Its only rules are those
it creates for its own purposes. The highest principle of

any revolutionary action, and therefore also Lenin's highest principle, is the aim. Primarily, the aim is the revolution itself; secondarily, it is the ideal state which is to be achieved through the revolution.[3]

His determination to usher in the revolution and his strategy of political advance led Lenin to postulate formation of a "cadre party" of professional revolutionaries. Since 1902 Lenin had opposed the idea of revolution generated spontaneously by the proletariat. He was unwilling to depend on any mythical factor, be it the independent, anonymous activity of history on behalf of the exploited or the automatic progress of the consciousness of the exploited themselves. Revolution must be organized purposefully. For that end the party is needed. It would consist of a minority who were truly class-conscious because of their training. Such a party would be able to lead the masses, as long as it is able to answer each pressing political question that arises.

It is not difficult to see that this principle of having an educated minority guide the proletariat, a principle based on a desire for efficiency, could also be applied to the Party itself. Consequently, Lenin demands the installation of "a strong, authoritative organ" for the Party, "a party centre which will have the general confidence of the party membership." And from the rank and file of the Party he will demand an "iron discipline, bordering [on] military discipline." Lenin thus formulates the cadre principle; it is his considered and noteworthy answer to the question of organization which poses itself to *all* movements: "The task is to create, to support and to strengthen a party nucleus which will lead the party out of the decomposition, disintegration and wavering that we see today, onto a solid path."[4] "Forces are being spared by a homogenous, closed organization, which is unanimous in questions of principle, not by gluing together dissimilar elements."[5]

Except for the aim, Lenin's so-called ethic is completely relativistic. It is a situation ethic based on the principle of revolution. Every action is conditioned by the particular situation and by the purpose—revolutionary change.

In 1920, in a speech before the Communist Youth Movement of the Soviet Union, Lenin spoke about the question raised by Sombart and others: Is there such a thing as a Communist morality? Of course, Lenin said, there is a Communist morality. But it is not like the morality of the bourgeoisie, which is oriented toward eternal laws handed down from heaven. "We say, our morality is completely subjected to the interests of the proletarian class struggle. Our morality is derived from the proletarian class struggle.... We subordinate our morality to this task. We say, anything is moral which serves the destruction of the old exploiters' society and the alliance of all working people around the proletariat which builds the new, the community society."[6]

With classical acumen and simplicity Lenin teaches a functional ethic, an ethic dependent on one overriding aim and on the different junctures of the road to reach it. The relativism of this action theory is expressed in sentences such as: "In politics there exists no morality, only expediency." And its relation in principle to the respective situation is made clear in Lenin's doctrine: "We must understand to adapt our tactics and our immediate tasks to the peculiarities of each given situation."[7]

Consequently, this almost absolute situation ethic does not attempt to prescribe beforehand, in a timeless fashion, how to act. Each situation is new, so there can be no eternal, universal laws. There is only the aim as the principle whose application differs with every passing second. This is reflected in the famous saying attributed to Communist playwright Bertolt Brecht: "A Communist must be able to keep a pact or to break a pact." Except for the goal, nothing is in itself good or evil. Everything depends on the situation and on its relation to the goal. Lenin postulates absolute freedom for revolutionary action.

This means that at times it may become necessary to make compromises, including perhaps making an alliance with a declared enemy. Lenin explains this with the following example:

> In 1918 when the German imperialist bandits threw their armies into defenseless Russia ... I hesitated not in the least to work for a certain agreement with French monarchists. The French officer de Lubersac was brought to meet me. "I am a monarchist," he declared. "My only aim is the overthrow of Germany.... " This did not prevent me from coming to terms with him concerning certain services which these French officers, experts with explosives, were willing to render us by blowing up railway lines, in order to stop the German invasion. That was the model of an "agreement" which every class-conscious worker will approve of, an agreement in the interest of socialism. The French monarchist and myself, we shook hands, although we knew that each would have loved to have the other one hanged. But our interests coincided in passing. Against the attacking German brigands we in the interest of the Russian and international socialist revolution made use of the evenly rapacious counter-interests of the other imperialists.... We made use of the method to maneuver, to attack and withdraw, which is absolutely legitimate and inevitable in any war. [8]

"The end justifies the means"—here one recognizes the guiding principle of all of post-Lenin, Soviet world politics, including the incredible pact between Hitler and Stalin in 1940. That pact was an extreme application of this principle, applied by both sides. The only question remaining after that pact was which party would be just a little cleverer in the act of deceiving the other one.

In another place Lenin explained the relationship between the overall aim and the immediate situation with the memorable paradox that one must now howl with the wolves, knowing that later all wolves must be extermi-

nated to bring about a truly human society.[9]
The concept of "peaceful coexistence" between different political systems can be found in Lenin's writings as the application of this principle of tactical and temporary compromise. Of course this was not meant to signal the end of class struggle and the renunciation of the aim to export revolution to capitalist countries. In fact, Soviet party leaders continuously express to rank-and-file members of the party—and also to all others who have ears to hear—that temporary peace does not mean they have given up their goal. In the context of Lenin's strategy the catch phrase *peaceful coexistence* means that immediate confrontation with foreign enemies is avoided so that interior strength can be rebuilt or so that attention can be given to another field of battle.[10]

Another classic example of this is the 1918 peace treaty with the German empire which Lenin signed at Brest-Litovsk under bitter and humiliating circumstances. Then he even accepted the cession of large territories because he regarded the battle on the interior front, for example, over the question of what position the peasantry would take, as more important. At that moment, internal turmoil demanded all his interest and all the available forces. Lenin explained that capitulation may be responsible action, if it is "the refusal to fight under obviously unfavourable conditions."[11]

As we know, the Soviet Union has long since won back those territories it lost at Brest-Litovsk. For Lenin, above the situation and above all forced compromises stands the aim to which he knows he must remain true.[12] It is obvious that in this sense Lenin's political principle has also become the basic motif of military guerilla strategy.

The Postrevolutionary Morality
Once the revolution was secured, however, we find Lenin supporting very different standards of morality. We can see these same standards in Soviet Party literature today.

Soviet Marxism does not invest its fortune in the idea of *permanent* revolution. In fact, it rejected this idea with the expulsion from the Soviet Union of one of the former leaders of the revolution, Leonid Trotsky, in 1927. The revolution rather appears as a one-time event, a turnover in history after which conditions consolidate.

This conception in turn generates a corresponding ethic. If the revolutionary ethic was relativistic, as the upheaval of time and the time of upheaval seemed to demand, so the new state of affairs demanded a different morality as a lasting basis for future development. A definite content of ethics was required to produce a steady and ordered society.

In his book *State and Revolution* (1917), Lenin looked into the future and tried to depict how society would develop in the time *after* the revolution. He writes, "Liberated men will by and by get accustomed to keeping the elementary rules of social and corporate life, which are known from old and have been preached . . . for thousands of years."[13] The surprising thing here is that Lenin matter-of-factly suddenly assumes that there is a stock of timeless, moral norms which all people are aware of and will keep. "Down with relativism!" he seems to be saying. From now on there are fixed norms valid for everyone and binding in all postrevolutionary situations.

Lenin himself draws attention to the change from revolutionary to postrevolutionary ethics. In 1918 he exhorted workers: "Keep account of money exactly and conscientiously! Do not steal! Observe the strictest discipline in your work." He supported this with a general statement which is quite revealing: "Those watchwords which revolutionary proletarians laughed at . . . when the bourgeoisie used them to cover up its domination, now become the most imminent and important watchwords after the dethronement of the bourgeoisie."[14]

A closer look at this statement reveals again the historical determination of ethics—different ethics for different situations. After the revolution, however, no further reversal of history and no further change in norms of action was to be expected, for Marxists defined all history as a "history of class wars," and history essentially comes to its end with the revolution that is to abolish class wars.

On the basis of Lenin's statement in *State and Revolution*, one could even conclude that the revolutionary ethos which threw out all traditional rules of social and corporate life was meant only for the exceptional situation. That situation would constitute a time exempt from the "elementary rules" valid at all other times, the mere *intermezzo* or interlude of revolution.

It is worth noting in passing that, when Lenin proclaimed the validity of certain norms for people living after the revolution, he was apparently refusing to put his confidence in the utopian idea of the inevitability of the "new man." A new species of man who spontaneously, without any outside instruction, does good and socially needed deeds, was supposed to be the end product of the revolution. But Lenin seems to have felt that rules were needed even after the revolution. Human nature, being what it is, needs a process of habituation, training in moral consciousness and instruction in ethics. In the same way the famous Russian educator Makarenko in the twenties postulated a Communist ethic. To him, it was indispensable for the education of the younger generation.[15]

In line with Lenin's prediction and instruction there took place in the Soviet Union after World War 2 a rapid quantitative growth in the number of students studying ethics and in the number of university chairs of ethics. Also, a change of viewpoint is evident. The leading role played by the political interests of the day vanishes, and many scholars return to the basic themes of morality.[16]

The rejection of a morality "derived from some supernatural, classless concept," as Lenin had voiced it in his speech before the Communist Youth Movement, is replaced by what might almost be termed a resurrected natural law. Thus the standard Marxist textbook on ethics by A. F. Schischkin presents us with adages which are well known from the ancient Greeks. For example, Schischkin says that "treaties must be kept" and immediately comments that the Soviet Union had always kept its treaties absolutely, punctually and meticulously.[17] The rapprochement with the timeless rules of morality as predicted by Lenin has been effected. Any action theory claiming the right to decide what to do on the basis of the situation, be it in accordance with or against traditional rules, is out of the question.

So there obviously are two types of ethics in Leninism, a revolutionary ethos and a postrevolutionary ethic, and both are arranged sequentially. Lenin's system, however, is susceptible to the criticism of those who say that the revolutionary ethos then will be valid for other countries, while the static morality is taught within the Communist power bloc. Or worse, critics accuse the Communists of saving the revolutionary ethic for the Party nucleus, while making the rank and file of the Party and the general population abide by the rules. They drive home the point that in the same way that demands for disciplined work were used by the bourgeoisie, today the Party uses the new normative ethics in the Soviet Union as a tool of domination: making sure that the workers behave in a disciplined and regular manner, and deleting any idea of change of the status quo from the consciousness of the people.

Applications of the Revolutionary Ethos
"The elementary rules . . . known from old" may not, when represented by Soviet ethics, yield much new perspective to the student of Christian ethics. On the other hand, the rarely undertaken study of Lenin's revolutionary "ethic," used for comparison, might grant us further insights into the present state and the future task of Christian ethics. As the examples will show, this is not just a matter of ethical theorizing, but of life.

For Lenin, the prime principle of revolutionary action was the aim. He said: Our morality is completely subordinated to the tasks set by the class struggle. From this it follows that there can be no neutral areas in the life of the individual fighter. There are no aspects of life which are independent of the rule of the purpose: that is, all aspects of life must be subordinate to our final goal. Lenin made this very clear when in conversation with Clara Zetkin, leader of the Communist women of Germany, he illustrated his point by demanding the subordination of sex under the Communist aim. "You know that young Comrade X. He is a splendid fellow, quite brilliant. I fear, nevertheless, that he will fail to live up to the promise. He whizzes and staggers from one womanizing story to the other. That isn't fit for the political battle, and for the revolution!" And again, "I do not bet on the dependability and perseverance in battle of those women where the personal romance gets mixed up with politics. . . . That does not go together with the revolution."[18]

In the same conversation of 1920 Lenin criticized the "hypertrophy of the sexual, observed so often nowadays." The overemphasis on sexuality did not grant joy and strength for living, but took it away. However, it is not this result which most concerned him. His ideal certainly was not the average middle-class standard of careful enjoyment of life's pleasures. Rather, he thought the demands of excessive sexual activity to be particularly dangerous in an age of revolution, "because revolution [and here he comes back to his primary theme] requires concentration and intensification of forces, both of the masses and of individuals."[19] The highest loyalty is to the revolution, and that goes for *private life* too. Is this single-mindedness and determination something which Christians could emulate?

From the same perspective Lenin also condemned the "damaging effect" of the "glass-of-water-theory" propagated by leading Communists and radical liberals at the beginning of the century. That theory said that exercising the sexual urge was no different from drinking a glass of water to quench the thirst. It simply satisfied a need. In his criticism of this theory Lenin condemned the unsocial element in it. It takes the other person merely as a means for physical gratification. But even more Lenin deplored the way in which this theory diverted all attention to instant sex and away from the political battle. All energy had to be claimed for the revolution.[20]

This same value is voiced by leaders in Red China today. Everyone must give his or her best years for the reconstruction of the nation. Early marriage is discouraged.

It is intriguing to note that Lenin not only rejected the demands of a free sex life, but also found no value in a "free" intellectual life—that is, one not disciplined by the overall purpose. Of writers who became members of the Party he would demand the same loyalty and determination as of other members. They could not go on as before, writing whatever happened to come to mind or whatever served to enhance their personal glory in the public eye.[21] Each move, every decision was to stand in relation to the perspective of the final purpose: The ethical is what serves the destruction of the old and the construction of the new society.

All thinking and action is directed toward the aim. Can you imagine a revolutionary who maintains certain areas of his or her life exempt from the overall purpose or in opposition to it? Lenin demanded a totality of commitment from the revolutionary. When Lenin spoke to a number of businessmen in Bern, Switzerland, before World War 1, he is said to have told them: "I have not invited you here because I want to have your free weekends. I am asking for your unlimited support."

The degree of commitment to the aim also determines the shaping and the limits of interpersonal relationships. "We recognize indeed," writes Lenin, "the duty of comradeship, the duty to support all comrades. But for us the duty of comradeship results from our duty to international Democratic Socialism (the name then used for the Leninist movement) and not the other way round."[22] This means that loyalty to the aims of the revolution must, if necessary, break the loyalty to an individual comrade and even abandon to the enemy former comrades who have become liabilities. The end justifies even this means. This was stated early by Lenin in theory and was practiced in internal Party fights around 1910.

Bertolt Brecht in his *Lehrstück: Die Massnahme* tried to justify this ethic when he describes a team of Communist agents who decide to liquidate a young comrade (and even demand his approval of the act) by pushing him into a pit of unslaked lime because he has let himself be recognized by the police. It was this principle of international Communism at which Arthur Koestler took offense, as we gather from his famous novel *Darkness at Noon*.

The complete, unbroken dominion of the chosen purpose produces the principle of strict partiality. It likewise demands that party comradeship must never be used to further the personal aims of any individual. This principle may be meaningful. However, if it is not limited by absolute moral standards preserving the life of the individual, the leadership may, as we have seen, sacrifice human lives as it sees fit. The absolute subordination of all action to the one aim may be amoral and destructive.

Lenin's Life as Paradigm
So far we have looked at some general principles of Lenin's revolutionary action theory. In spite of his emphasis on the context-relatedness of ethical decisions, he still maintained belief in a formal ethos, a kind of revolutionary "exhortation." Yet because the emphasis is on relativity (when the revolutionary rule is applied to particular situations many different actions may be prescribed), the best way to demonstrate this type of ethic would be by way of

paradigm, by giving examples of the revolutionary life.[23] Relating stories of how revolutionaries actually acted will help to avoid meaningless abstractions. Therefore this method is used in the Soviet Union where the biographies of revolutionary prototypes of the new society are held to be an important educational tool.

Lenin also used this method. He set forth the example of Babushkin, one of his professional revolutionaries: "Always active among the workers, he sets up study circles, organizes libraries, and continues to learn devotedly himself."[24]

The simple indicative of a concrete illustration can have an effect stronger than many imperatives. This format is possible where, because of the overarching purpose, motivation otherwise coming by way of an imperative order may be taken for granted. In Soviet literature Lenin himself is often the archetype of the revolutionary and of the so-called new man.[25] And indeed the conduct of this eminent revolutionary as well as his writings demonstrate the essential elements of his revolutionary ethos. Let us look at how he shaped his life in accordance with the one purpose in different situations, including before the revolution, in deportment and exile.

During the first phase (1894-95) of his party activity Lenin in Petersburg read Marx's *Capital,* the classic book of Marxism, with a group of workers. At the same time, Krupskaya, his companion, organized a Marxist group among her schoolteacher colleagues.[26] Both emphasized the principle of forming study groups. "Agitation," that is, teaching (catechesis) was being stressed throughout and won additional weight when linked to the problems of the working day. Lenin also urged such action by pointing to the need for constant contact with the masses of ordinary people. Lenin wanted to reach out to them and to establish close contact with them to win them to his side.[27] Continued communication with ordinary men and women was indispensable for the work of the revolutionary intellectual.

In addition to these study groups, there was another activity which was important to Lenin at this time. This was the exchange of letters with imprisoned revolutionaries. During his own deportation to Siberia (1897-1900), when his revolutionary activity suffered from outward limitations, one of the tasks Lenin undertook was to set up legal counseling for the other deportees and so built up his prestige in the new surroundings. At the same time (under the comparatively easy conditions of tsarism!), he was able to handle an extensive correspondence and to undertake an intense study of Party literature. He found that during a time when one is cut off from the forefront of the battle, personal discipline becomes important in order to avoid privatization and slackening of the revolutionary pace. His motto was to refrain from everything which detracted from revolutionary fighting.[28]

As soon as Lenin was free again, having fled from Siberia to exile in Western Europe, he again began to travel and to work for the cause. Traveling was necessary in order to make contacts with other revolutionaries. Lenin's guideline was that the strength of a revolutionary organization consists in the number and quality of its connections. He illustrated this with an example: Babushkin made regular rounds of the places where work had previously been done in order to strengthen contacts with the revolutionaries.[29]

About three hundred letters per month were sent into tsarist Russia from the Communist cell group in Geneva. Also in Geneva they produced a newspaper in Russian which was smuggled into Russia from various directions, in ever-new disguises by mail or through merchants and sailors.[30]

Further tasks arose at times of confusing temporary failure of the Party. From Krupskaya's memoirs we see that Lenin, during such periods of "revolutionary depression," paid particular attention to "upholding the honor, the prestige and the continuity of the Party."[31] This he effected in Geneva, for example, by organizing "jours fixes," weekly meetings aimed at helping the revolutionaries close their ranks around the common purpose. He felt it was of paramount importance to meet together regularly and to live together.[32]

At that moment, when the success of the revolution seemed far off, the Party had to be rebuilt. That was the time for literary activity. Lenin worked assiduously at this himself and drew others into it as well. Scattered believers, the Diaspora, can often be gathered by way of literature. So Lenin began with pamphlets and later moved on to producing a newspaper. During these years of disintegration of the Party organization, the most important front was ideological. Lenin stated somewhat paradoxically that fights between factions are a sign of vigor and strength in the Party. Many popularly written articles were needed to clarify the questions of the day. A large publishing program got under way.[33]

Simply by virtue of the volume of its literature production, Lenin's group developed a superiority which made it a focal point for the revolutionaries in dispersion. This was exactly what Lenin intended. This is why he allegedly said that he would rather write a brochure than speak at twenty mass rallies. In a time of crisis the main emphasis must go to gathering and strengthening the revolutionaries.

We can hardly examine these elements of Lenin's life without being repeatedly confronted by the similarity—and dissimilarity—between his life and the life of a Christian missionary. In both individual elements and basic structures, such as the totality of commitment, we can see parallels. Revolutionary ethics by its very nature is an "ethics" of exodus, both in terms of history and geography. It is the instruction for establishing new conditions. As such, revolutionary ethics stands side by side with the ethics of preservation and maintenance of (for example, natural) conditions. The very juxtaposition, however, of these two types of ethics in Lenin is sufficient to challenge us to re-examine the overall structure of our own, Christian ethics.

In the next chapter we will look at the various ways in which Leninism challenges Christian ethics in general and the lives of individual Christians in particular. These challenges arise in relation to purpose, exodus, situation-directedness, consciousness of history and the distinction between the ethics of revolution and of preservation.

Chapter 7

The Challenge to Christian Ethics

I t must be understood from the start that in Christian ethics we speak in terms of purposes given by God rather than set up by humans.

A look through the more popular textbooks on ethics, both Protestant and Roman Catholic, leads us to the conclusion that Christian ethics is traditionally conceived of as an ethics of creation order or natural law. Most treatments of ethics include chapters on marriage and the family, vocation and society, the state, and perhaps a chapter on the church. In a somewhat flat, timeless manner, traditional ethics describe the ordinary way of human action in the world. The eschatological horizon of the Christian life rarely comes into focus, and, where it does, it is so formalized that it seldom motivates Christian action or determines its context in any measure. The concept of ethics being centered on a single purpose is not a well-known idea.

The Great Commission for Today

It is helpful, therefore, to examine our concept of ethics as well as the practical formation of our lives in terms of aim and purpose: What are we living for? The New Testament has a better view of this than the theological textbooks both past and present.

The biblical concept which is equivalent to the Marxist notion of purpose or aim is the concept of mission. Christ's Great Commission is the central perspective and the aim set for the life of the Christian. It is spelled out in Matthew 28:18-20: "All authority in heaven and on earth has been given to me. Go therefore and make disciples of all nations, baptizing them in the name of the Father and of the Son and of the Holy Spirit, teaching them to observe all that I have commanded you; and lo, I am with you always, to the close of the age." This is paralleled in Colossians 1:27-29, which states that Christ is "in you, the hope of glory. Him we proclaim, warning every man and teaching every man in all wisdom, that we may present every man mature in Christ. For this I toil, striving with all the energy which he mightily inspires within me."[1] Both formulas indicate the universalism of the commission and the totality of commitment which it demands.

The aim of mission, then, may be described in different ways. According to Colossians 1:28 it should be defined as the nurture of humanity in the image of Christ. This is almost an earlier analogy to the Marxist concept of the humanization of man and the educational work needed toward that end. Just as Christ lived in complete obedience to the kingship of God, so the Christian's aim is to establish God's kingship in the world. The kingdom of God is the end of and the framework for Christian ethics.

It is interesting how well Marxists seem to understand the centrality and exclusiveness of the kingdom of God for the Christian faith. This can be seen, for instance, in the Soviet demand that Aleksandr Solzhenitsyn replace the capital "G" in God in one of his manuscripts with a small letter before publication. It is also seen in the following anecdote: A few years ago the Brethren Church in Rumania was given permission to reprint their hymn book. They were requested, however, to purge from all songs the references to Jesus as Lord and to his present or future kingdom. Moreover, the concept of King had to be replaced by the title of Savior.[2] One is almost reminded of the trouble early Christianity had with the Roman authorities (and vice versa). It is the biblical idea of God's kingdom which makes any existing form of absolute government nervous.

The rule of God is the aim of Christian ethics. Consciousness of purpose will always create a dynamic ethic which cannot be reduced to merely maintaining existing conditions. It creates an ethic which is also in keeping with the fact that truth reaches its aim only through conflict and the overcoming of antagonism.

Missions understood comprehensively as the realization of the kingdom of God in the lives of men and women —"Your will be done on earth as it is being done in heaven"—is the aim to which traditional Christian ethics needs to be directed. As long as the only distinctly Christian element in Christian ethics is thought to be the different motivation for the same moral actions required equally from everyone, the doubt raised since the Reformation that Christian ethics may not be distinct in content will remain.

In his old age Karl Barth took the bold step of writing an ethic of the "order of reconciliation" for Christians to supplement the creation ethic which applies to all people. He was able to finish and publish only a fragment of this, however: the doctrine of baptism in the incomplete fourth volume (part 4) of his *Church Dogmatics*.[3] He might have gone on to unfold the Great Commission as the framework for this distinctively Christian part of ethics.

The Great Commission is the first and foremost imperative of Christian ethics. It connects the elements of exodus and of regeneration. In a truly Christian ethical system the theological foundation of foreign missions would at last be established. Until now, judging by most current manuals of Christian ethics, the missionary commission has been assumed to be irrelevant to the average Christian. In a similar fashion, the theology of missions has often not been included in the overall scheme of theological science.

Christian ethics must become conscious again of its given purpose. The purpose simultaneously constitutes a *functional* personal discipline. Piety which is not oriented toward the world horizon and the task of changing people —both aspects of the missionary commission—easily becomes sterile. The same is true for the work of theoretical ethics.

We need to grasp and exercise the insight that the Christian's task is not exhausted by living a decent life according to the creational order. We must learn to dedicate our lives to the larger commission of God's kingdom with the same consciousness and purposiveness, circumspection and energy that we have seen in Lenin. This means we must rid ourselves of amateurish attitudes and irrelevant lifestyles.

Very often we benefit from the gospel like sparrows who during the winter enjoy the warmth from our heated homes, but do not concern themselves with the heating. Sparrows, of course, are intended to be free of responsibility. Christians are not. Lenin's militancy may remind us of the early Christian virtue of *militia Christi*, the soldierly service of Christ. Toward the end of soldierly service we must daily and hourly orient and adjust our actions.

The Exodus Principle
The Christian life is characterized by a constant exodus from old habits and conditions. Like Paul, the Christian is

always "forgetting what lies behind and straining forward to what lies ahead, . . . [pressing] on toward the goal for the prize of the upward call of God in Christ Jesus" (Phil. 3:13-14). The Christian's life resembles—something we tend to forget under the influence of mere creation ethics —a pilgrimage. Christians are pilgrims on the road, and they have not yet attained their lasting home.

The missionary commission adds another level of exodus. It is not by chance that Christ's Great Commission begins with the commandment, "Go therefore. . . ." World mission is incomprehensible without the practical application of the principle of exodus from one's present state and condition. Missionaries need mobility. But this does not pertain only to missionaries in the technical sense; that is, those who work in full-time, cross-cultural missions. This can be seen from the fact that Abraham, who was the first to leave his country and his kindred upon God's command (Gen. 12:1), was made the example of all believers because of his willingness to obey. Furthermore, the Exodus of Israel from Egypt became the model for the church of the new covenant. The Exodus provided an example of practical obedience in the exercise of the missionary commission and in persecution.

In the Old Testament, God's messengers were taken away from their traditional occupations and lifestyles. The prophet Amos expressed this when he said: "I am a herdsman, and a dresser of sycamore trees, and the LORD took me from following the flock, and the LORD said to me, 'Go, prophesy to my people Israel' " (7:14-15). Jesus himself left his home and his family, so that he no longer had a place to call his own: "Foxes have holes, and birds of the air have nests; but the Son of man has nowhere to lay his head" (Mt. 8:20). His exodus had deeper meaning in that he left the Father's presence for the sake of returning to his presence those who had fallen out of it. Christ himself is the Good Shepherd who will leave the ninety-nine sheep in the pasture in order to seek the one which was lost (Mt. 18:12). His is an exodus from well-settled domestic life undertaken for love's sake. Like Jesus, his disciples could speak about having left for his sake not only their nets, their occupations and possessions, but also their fathers and mothers, wives and children (Mt. 19:29).

Jesus' disciples, with their mobility and availability, are the prototype for the professional revolutionaries called for by Lenin. Availability is the characteristic of the cadres. Until the growth of world missions in the nineteenth and twentieth centuries, it was the monks and nuns who particularly represented the exodus from civil life in the history of Christianity: they were the ones who looked after the call to missions and charity, as the two foremost fields of special Christian ethics. To be sure, the renunciation or sacrifice of family, security and possessions, mentioned in Matthew 19, is the special vocation of individuals. But we must not use this to blind ourselves to the fact that availability and mobility for service in God's kingdom is demanded of all Christians. Christians are called "saints" in the New Testament. Being a saint means foremost being "available for God." In general, the Great Commission is for all of Christ's disciples, and vocation, as Barth has rightly emphasized, goes beyond occupation.[4]

Ethics In and Out of Time

The way that ethical decisions for Lenin are related to the particular historical situation presents a challenge to conventional Christian ethics in two different ways. First, a comparison with Lenin exposes the overall lack in Christianity of a consciousness of history both in ethical instruction and in actual practice. Insofar as Lenin's world view presupposes the Marxist thesis, "All history is a history of class wars," so Christian ethics ought to recognize its historical presupposition, "All history is a history of the battle for the realization of God's kingdom." Among the textbooks of Christian ethics that are available today, only the ethics of Paul Lehmann seems to approach a similar perspective.

Lehmann describes Christian ethics as "context ethics."[5] The context which is to be observed in Christian decision making, however, for Lehmann is no longer the realm of the creational order, but the life of the church. Yet even with this improvement, Christian ethics as seen by Lehmann does not lose the peculiar character of *timelessness* that is so common to many ethics textbooks. Past ethicists had often added the category of *church* (almost as a kind of surrogate for eschatology) to the timeless categories of creation ethics, such as marriage, the family, society and the state. But when the church was treated in this way it was conceived of as a static, unchanging entity. In contrast to this, the church should be seen as a dynamic force moving within history. Only when we begin to understand the kingdom of God as a process running within human history, can we properly speak of contextual Christian ethics which takes into account not only the coordinate of space, but also of time.

With this we come to the second challenge Leninist ethics issues to Christianity. Traditional Christian ethics, as has been said, have had a timeless character, representing the creational ordinances of God. Reformational ethics, stressing the eternal validity of the Ten Commandments, allowed for only one adaptation of ethics to an individual's situation. Distinctions in ethics could, according to Luther, be made on the basis of vocation and considerations of the natural cycles intrinsic to certain vocations, such as the seasonal differences in a farmer's work or the phases in pregnancy and child rearing.[6] Beyond that, this ethic was timeless.

After the Reformation the need for further specialization of moral instruction, brought back to Protestantism the method of casuistry, well known (and formerly despised) in Catholic moral theology. Casuistry is the practice of applying general ethical norms in advance to possible situations and cases in order to derive somewhat more specific rules. When this was done, if one remained unsatisfied with casuistry—which one well might—the rest was left to human reason. So traditional Protestant ethics was reduced to the Decalogue plus a few exhortations regarding varying roles in society taken from the New Testament.[7] The actual situation remained empty of concrete instructions for action.

The Search for a New Morality

The so-called New Morality was a rebellion in the 1960s against this obvious inability of traditional morality to specify action in concrete situations. Its initiators, Joseph Fletcher and John A. T. Robinson, reacted against the inadequacy in traditional ethics by proposing a pure ethic of the situation, doing away with universal norms altogether.[8] The New Morality's radical proposals were sure to capture headlines. Robinson's idea, that he would like to see his children equipped for the future with a built-in moral compass, has some fascinating parallels to the Old Testament promise of a new person with a new heart, able to discern right and wrong (Jer. 31:33-34; Ezek. 36:27). But a more careful consideration reveals imperfections in the New Morality that are no more pardonable than those of traditional ethics.[9]

The New Morality's reduction of ethics to private, individual decisions, its preoccupation with sex and its generally quite limited horizon cannot be overlooked.[10] The complete absence of a superior aim is evident. The New Morality is an antinomian situation ethic, *within* the already too narrow horizons of the old morality (that is, the creational, domestic existence outlined by traditional ethics). It lacks an emphasis on the exodus motif and a concern for the missionary commission. It lacks creativity. A truly Christian ethic would not be satisfied with learning how to adapt successfully to a given situation, but would for the sake of its purpose be willing to break up existing situations and leave them behind.

So the New Morality is not a solution to the problems we found in the old morality. The call to missions requires an ethic which can be related to each new situation on the basis of its overall aim.[11] Now if it is agreed that the challenge of Lenin's revolutionary ethic must be met and that the New Morality is inadequate to meet it, then it can be seen that what is needed is a *purposive* situational ethic.

However, for such an ethic there remains the question of who or what is to decide just *how* the overall aim must be applied to an individual situation to determine the appropriate action. In Catholicism this difficulty has been solved by making particular *persons* responsible for relating the Christian purpose to the situation. The history of monasticism shows that *hierarchy* is the principle of authority which is constituted by the vow of obedience the individual monk makes to his abbot. In the history of Marxism, Lenin's postulate of an authoritative Party center has produced a similar structure. This principle applied seems often to lead to the rule of *one* personality (although the necessity of spontaneity is affirmed in theory) and the degeneration of the hierarchical principle to a personality cult.

In the New Testament, looking at the gathering described in Acts 15, one might on first view be inclined to think in terms of a group analogous to the Party center. But the New Testament limits the authority of those who lead. Their authority is restricted by the instruction of the invisible chief Shepherd (1 Pet. 5:4) and by the incalculable horizon of God's kingship. In a way somewhat similar to what we have heard from Lenin, Paul, the new apostle, sets the plan of the kingdom before the consideration of personalities, be they colleagues or even "pillars of the church." For example, in Galatians 2:11-21, Paul reprimanded the apostle Peter for acting hypocritically with regard to the Jewish laws and their importance for gentile Christians.

It seems that in the New Testament, the decisive factor in the interpretation of the situation and the action demanded by it is not human reason. Wherever reason alone claims authority, a tyranny of a few people over many develops and with it the many tragic results that are observed in the history of revolutions. Due to the limitations of human reason, different people will assess each situation in different ways, and friction and rebellion will result. Human reason alone is inadequate for the task of interpretation·

The Christian faith sees the Holy Spirit as the authority for the interpretation of the situation. He is the leader of those who fight for the realization of the kingdom of God. The guidance of the Holy Spirit is the practical unfolding of the kingdom of God, which remains an abstract concept without it. Similarly, the Christian mission is incomprehensible without the instruction of the Holy Spirit.[12] The voice of the Spirit marked the beginning of the systematic mission to the heathen: "Set apart for me Barnabas and Saul for the work to which I have called them" (Acts 13:2).

Whoever would speak of the kingdom of God must recapture the doctrine of the Holy Spirit. The Word of the Spirit as the interpretation of the kingdom is central for Christian ethics. It is by the Word of the Spirit that we determine our actions in each situation according to the purposes of God. We ourselves cannot effect the transformation of humanity into the image of Christ. We seek merely to make ourselves available as God's fellow workers (1 Cor. 3:9).

Two Kinds of Ethics

To my mind, the most fundamental challenge resulting from Lenin's action theory for the study of Christian ethics lies in the indication of two different levels of action, one revolutionary and one non(post)revolutionary. It is immediately clear that the ethics of the Bible corresponds to this structure—there are two levels of action. Yet these two levels do not, as they do for Lenin, correspond to different periods of time, one following the other, or to different groups of people. Rather, both forms of ethics fall into the same time, one supplementing the other. The extraordinary (revolutionary) act of the Christian, especially of the missionary (or, indeed, of every Christian with regard to his missionary concern), has its place above and beyond (but not outside of) the creational ordinances of God, as represented by traditional ethics.

Thus, Christian situation ethics under the horizon of the kingdom of God accepts situational relativism *only within the boundaries of the Ten Commandments.* By this it avoids the arbitrariness of an action determined purely by the acting subject, and it evades the absolute rule of man over man which always results from such subjectivism. This illuminates the deep meaning of Paul's saying, "Where the Spirit of the Lord is, there is freedom" (2 Cor. 3:17), that is to say: freedom from the tyranny of men.

Christian and Marxist Ethics in Conflict

In our study we have found significant analogies between Marxist-Leninist and Christian ethics. Yet our final conclusion must be that the two ethics are very different. Although both emphasize a central purpose, the need to forsake the past and a functional concept of action, they have very *different* aims. And although both have a strong concern for the situation and an awareness of historical development, they maintain these within very different frameworks.

Therefore, the analogies between Marxist-Leninist and Christian ethics are of a formal nature.

The content of a purpose, however, inevitably determines every single detail of an ethic. One's ethics are always a reflection of one's world view. Marxism has throughout replaced the kingship of God with the unlimited dominion of man over the world. This aim then occasions the rejection of any framework of moral absolutes like the Ten Commandments or other common moral systems. This aim also has as its effect that all instructions for action in specific situations are based on purely human and rational considerations. The basic problem of Marxist ethics is its presupposed atheism. When applied to ethics, atheism results in titanic, unlimited authority of man over his actions.

This statement of the fundamental difference between Christianity and Marxism concerning the aim and the limits of action can finally provide us with the answer to the much-debated question of whether there can be cooperation between Christians and Marxists. Because of their presuppositions, it is clear that Marxism and Christianity cannot be thought of as complementing each other. Wherever such a union has nevertheless been attempted, Marxism gave the instructions for action and Christianity was reduced to motivational faith. This combination of elements can be found in various places. Recently, Bishop Krusche of East Germany described it as follows:

Cooperation of Christians and Marxists has often been called for in our society. In the practical work of our occupation it comes as a matter of course. In the realm of politics we often get the impression that our cooperation is desired, but not so that we could contribute something substantial of our own. What we may contribute as our own is only our peculiar motivation, and then it is supposed to be self-evident that we, although with the different motivation, in fact do exactly what the Party of the Working Class has already laid down. As a result we are meant to do the same as everybody else, only with a different motivation. The Gospel however, does not only provide us with impulse for action but also with criteria and material points of view which must be taken into consideration in our action. They may then lead to the same material solutions and decisions as the Marxists have made on the basis of their

presuppositions, but must *not necessarily do so.*[13]
The demand to reduce faith to a motivation for actions
suggested by someone else is also found in the West and
even deliberately proclaimed by some theologians.[14] But
we should by now have learned from past mistakes. This
marriage of Christianity with a system for action was tried
in Germany. As recently as 1933, German Christians, sup-
porters of National Socialism, argued for reducing Christianity to a motivation when they proclaimed: "Germany
our goal, Christ our strength!" But soon they realized they
were simply fellow travelers on a road to alien ends.

Against this it must be stated that faith and works must
be kept together. Where we allow them to be separated,
we justify both the notion of an inactive faith and the
amalgamation of faith with diverse political ideologies,
exactly what we blamed our forefathers for.

People who derive their actions from different purposes, will work together only in a limited way. Practically, Christians and Marxists may only be able to col-
laborate well on activities related to the immediate needs
of life. And even here one must be aware that Marxists
will—to an extent which Christians still have to learn—
always keep in mind their larger aims. In the case of political and military alliances this has sometimes led to a
"war within the war," a hidden fight against the present
ally as a possible future competitor for power. The Civil
War in Spain and the French resistance movement against
German occupation during World War 2, provide obvious
examples.[15]

Some people have said that if your house was burning
and a fellow came running with a bucket full of water you
would not first ask him to state his religious convictions.
Thus, we should not be concerned about religious and political convictions when we are recruiting forces to work
on world problems affecting human survival. But this illustration is misleading. When I am fighting to extinguish
a fire, I have the right and duty to check a volunteer's

bucket to make sure it does not contain gasoline. There are, indeed, sufficient examples in history of political strategists who would try to inflame a political conflict in order to bring about a more radical solution. Some people welcome a building fire because they hope to achieve a more complete and modern reconstruction of the destroyed building.

Christians and Marxists in working together would again and again run into difficulty in situations where Christians must point to the moral limitations of political action while Marxists might ignore these limitations for reasons of expediency.

Christians trained in the Bible could never adopt the complete ethical relativism of the motto governing Marxist-Leninist action, "The end justifies the means." They would find it irresponsible to do evil in order that good may come out of it, for example, to preach hatred against the class enemy where the brotherhood of all people is supposed to be the true eventual aim. Because of its atheism and its consequences Marxism-Leninism is for Christians an unacceptable form of socialism.

This, of course, does not preclude cooperation in questions concerning the maintenance of life, within the bounds of God's commandments and particularly on a communal level, where major political strategy is less of a burden.

All these considerations lead to one conclusion. We need a theory of social ethics for Christians, one which will be generally intelligible and compatible with basic Christian beliefs. In the work of maintaining life, a task to which Christians are commissioned by God's creational ordinances, believers may work together with anyone who is willing to work as long as the work is compatible with biblical standards.[16]

Therefore, it is necessary that, especially where evangelical social ethics is at stake, we should act with sobriety and think clearly and rigorously. We must abandon the sentimentality which falls over itself in an effort to make up for past inadequacies. Our sinful, inadequate past needs to be cleared by forgiveness and change rather than being kept afloat by emotional blackmail. Above all, as Christians we must recover an awareness of the Great Commission, the ultimate goal of the Christian life, of which we have been reminded in studying Lenin's revolutionary ethos. And we must apply it to all our actions.

Part IV

Creating the
New Man

Chapter 8

The New Man in Marxism and Christianity

The problem of the so-called New Man or the "new type of man" is the most central theme in the dialogue between Christians and Marxists. Many Christians, however, and many Marxists are as yet largely unaware of the relevance of this subject for both world views.

Marxism and the New Man
Making use of a number of quotations from different sources we will try first to get some idea of the importance of this topic to Marxist thought. We shall look at the Marxist concept of the New Man and compare it to the Christian image of the new creature. We will then be able to move on to the subject of the genesis of the New Man in both Marxism and Christianity.

The concept in the beginnings of Marxism. In recent

years Marxism has become less dominated by the economic-materialist perspectives which characterized its history in the second half of the nineteenth century. There has been renewed interest in the anthropological problems which characterized Marx's early writings.

Marx criticized the French Revolution for having produced a political emancipation only and not the needed "human emancipation."[1] The revolution of 1789 gave political freedom to individual citizens, but did not make them true human beings who would live in brotherhood with others. Rather, it removed the barriers of egotism (for example, the economic egotism of the individual) and opened the door to its fuller development. Therefore, even after the French Revolution and its cry for brotherhood, man remained man's greatest enemy.

The need for a change in human nature to complement the changes in political structures is a common theme in Marxism from the beginning. In 1843 Ludwig Feuerbach wrote: "We need new men!"[2] The old ones were spiritually broken by centuries of bondage, which the abolition of absolute monarchy could not suddenly overcome. The removal of external serfdom is not sufficient to produce a free person. Marx responds to this problem in an important statement from his essay "On the Jewish Question": "Only when the real, individual man ... as an individual human being has become a *species* [social] *being* in his everyday life, in his particular work, and in his particular situation ..., only then will human emancipation have been accomplished."[3] Man must yet be liberated in order to arrive at humanity and brotherhood.

The focus on individuals and their everyday, practical ways of life provides a precise localization of that "human emancipation" which Karl Marx has in mind. Quoting the French philosopher-reformer Rousseau, Marx points out that the task is nothing less than "*changing*, so to speak, *human nature*, ... *transforming* each individual, who in himself, is a complete and solitary whole, into a *part* of a greater whole, ... of substituting a *partial* and *moral* [responsible] *existence* for physical and independent existence."[4] In short, Marx is looking for people who have left their ego-dominated pasts behind and have put the interests of humanity before their own.

The true and fundamental task, then, of the reformation of society consists of the emancipation of humanity from egotism—the liberation of each person from selfishness. The recognition of this as the central task of Marxism has never been completely lost. It was, however, hidden for some time when Marxism was mainly dominated by materialism. Nevertheless, statements such as "conditions make men just as much as men make conditions" can be found.[5] Humanity, therefore, would have to be changed along with the conditions.

Reappearance of the concept with Lenin. The concept of the New Man, although hidden for a long time, became a public issue again after the rise of Marxism-Leninism to power in Russia. In 1919 Lenin said, "The workers are building the new society without having turned themselves into new men who would be free from the dirt of the old world. They are still in it up to their knees." If they had waited for human nature to be changed before they began the revolution, then the Communists would have had to postpone social reconstruction to the distant future.[6]

Very soon, however, Lenin played a different tune. Obviously, the renewal of humanity could not be postponed indefinitely. In the deep distress of the civil-war winter of 1919-20, Lenin found himself confronted with a situation which almost demanded another revolution, this time a revolution of the spirit, in the hearts of men. This was not a romantic ideal for which the time had finally come, but a necessity for reasons of material survival. More than once we will find that the problem of the New Man is closely linked with the elementary economic needs of the society.

The problem was, as Lenin stated it, that in the present situation they were faced with a kind of vicious circle: "In order to raise per capita productivity, we must save ourselves from hunger, and in order to save ourselves from hunger we must raise the level of per capita productivity." Then he concluded his argument with a statement which at first glance looked rather astonishing, coming from a leading exponent of dialectical materialism: "As everybody knows, such antagonisms are solved in practice by the heroic initiative of individuals and of small groups which effects a reversal in the mood of the masses."[7]

Lenin here alluded to the so-called Communist *subbotniks*. In a difficult, almost desperate moment when people were too weak to increase production, but needed to increase production in order to no longer be weak, some conscientious workers of the Moscow-Kazan Railroad got together and on a free day put in a day's unpaid work. They even paid for the bowl of soup which was being provided. It was this unselfish, sacrificial heroic initiative, Lenin said, which effected a reversal in the general mood of the people, created confidence and encouraged additional efforts which were necessary to get them out of the economic cul-de-sac. At the same time, this type of voluntary work marked the actual beginning of Communism, because working for the sake of the needs of society, rather than for one's own sake or because one had to, is the true Communist way of work. Here the iron laws of the material possibilities of people still living egotistically are finally seen to be broken.[8]

The attributes of the New Man. After World War 2, Soviet educator V. Sukhomlinsky published a book entitled *The Education of Communist Man*. The book presents startling affirmations concerning the characteristics of the Marxist New Man. Two attributes in particular are stressed over a number of other qualities: spiritual self-reliance and a capacity for teamwork. "True Communists," writes Sukhomlinsky, "have an independence and a will power which do not in the first place result from decisions made by the collective." Only those who showed stability before their own consciences could be an example for the young generation to emulate. Individual strength and initiative counted more than merely obeying orders from the collective.

A structure of party loyalty coupled with individual responsibility was supposed to be the model of future Communist morality. Sukhomlinsky continues: "The most important motivation in a truly communist person is not the will of others, it is the ideal, his inner conviction." Communists, he says, are "people who in their actions are guided above all by their conscience. Such persons have already achieved Communism [the ideal state of society] as regards their moral development, they no longer need control over the amount of their work or their demands." Theirs is "an honesty in their innermost personal lives which at no time ever have been subject to the control of society, and never can be."[9]

As an example, Sukhomlinsky told the story of a worker who, faced with a bursting dam, risked his own life to save the lives of a large number of people. Asked for his motives, he had answered: "I did not wait for orders or advice but acted according to the needs of the circumstances. For me, this was an experience like a regeneration."

All this calls for comment. The concept of regeneration, well known from the New Testament, seems to surface in many places in the search for the New Man. The concept of conscience also appears frequently. To be "a conscientious worker" means to listen to one's conscience which, of course, is to be informed by the general directives of the Party. This is almost an atheistic parallel to the Christian doctrine of the consonance of Spirit and Scripture. After his heroic action, the worker in Sukhomlinsky's illustration went on to say that "My whole life changed. For I began to listen to my conscience. I understood that only he can be happy who fights and overcomes difficulties, not driven by coercion, but following his conscience. We will be able to move mountains when every worker becomes a conscious fighter."

Sukhomlinsky himself once again summed up this perspective with the statement: "Someone who has never yet taken a relevant step from his own conviction, cannot be a conscious creator of Communism. At best he is a disciplined performer of the will of others, but that does not suffice for the man of tomorrow."[10]

Self-reliance, spontaneity in doing good and the ability for teamwork are the basic qualities of the New Man. *Self-reliance* means following one's conscience as the necessary and fundamental source of moral insight.

Concern about the role of individual conscience was expressed by the writer of an article in the Moscow government daily, *Isvestya,* when he wrote about the preceding period of Soviet rule: "Think of the allegedly outdated idea of conscience! Knowledge of good and evil makes the difference between man and animal. The more painful and incomprehensible is it that this source of his very nature has been torn from him which really, as it were, was planted into him according to his description of service."[11]

The question is being raised whether conscience is not the very place to begin creating the new, selfless, responsible person. Today, this emphasis upon conscience takes on global relevance for Communism because formerly "monolithic" world Communism has splintered, and orders are no longer received from a single, authoritative center. Whenever there are several centers of authority, the final outcome depends upon each group doing the right thing on its own. One can no longer rely on bringing about the desired end by a dictate.

The literature of today tries to depict the true man of the future as an independent person. It contains some rather utopian concepts. The person of the future—according to the widely read natural scientist and author of utopian novels, Ivan Jefremov—is no longer a specialist in the bad sense of the word but "a universal expert possessing a sound and well-built body, a keen consciousness and capacity for thinking, together with exemplary moral qualities and an inner wealth of emotions."[12] Naturally, Jefremov is thinking here of an age one or two thousand years from now. But others are seeking this reality in the present and describe the qualities of their "positive heroes" as "trustworthiness, kindness, readiness to pardon and forgive, patience, modesty and purity of heart, sympathy with the suffering of others, loyalty to their aims, simplicity, wisdom of heart as opposed to mere cold intellect, courage, incorruptibility and firmness in their commitment to the truth."[13] Both the utopians and those who are concerned with the education of humanity see the New Man above all as a comrade of trustworthiness and kindness. It is the old idea of a combination of righteousness and love.

Finally, as the New Man, in the sense held by Soviet Marxists, is above all a moral person, so the twelve commandments of the "Moral codex of the builders of Communism" give us a good description of the nature of the New Man. This set of rules is part of the Program of the Communist Part of the Soviet Union (CPUSSR) of 1961 and includes the following principles:

    —loyalty to the cause of Communism, love for the Socialist homeland and for the Socialist countries,

    —conscientious work for the welfare of society: if a man will not work, he shall not eat,

    —care taken by each one for the preservation and increase of common property,

    —high social consciousness of duty, impatience against offenses against the common interest,

    —a spirit of collective and mutual comradely assistance: one for all, all for one,

    —humane attitude and mutual respect of all men: man is man's friend, comrade and brother,

–honesty and love of truth, moral purity, simplicity and modesty in social and personal life,

–mutual respect in the family, responsibility for the education of children,

–implacability regarding injustice, parasitism, dishonesty, careerism and greed,

–friendship and brotherliness of the peoples of the USSR, impatience toward national discord and race hatred,

–intransigence toward the enemies of Communism, peace, and the freedom of nations,

–fraternal solidarity with all workers of all countries, with all nations. [14]

The problem posed programmatically. In 1961, at the Twenty-Second Party Congress of the CPUSSR, the third Party program was adopted and interpreted by Nikita Khrushchev in a marathon speech. The text of the program and of his five-hour speech are of considerable value in understanding the nature of the so-called New Man.

In addition, Leonid Ilyichov, leading ideologist of the Khrushchev era, gave another major speech on the theme at the plenary meeting of the Central Committee of the CPUSSR in June 1963, which dealt with the question of ideology. Ilyichov described the New Man as follows: "A builder of Communism is a fully developed person, combining a rich intellect, moral integrity, mature aesthetic tastes, and physical perfection ... people who have remade themselves ... [with] new attitudes to labour and to one's social obligations, [with] a new kind of discipline ..., new moral principles, ... self-discipline, and moral purity." "Unity of word and deed" and "a living spirit of Party creativeness" are required.

About the education of the New Man, Ilyichov said: "The Party considers the education of the new man to be the most difficult task in the Communist transformation of society. ... Unless we uproot the moral principles of the bourgeois world, educate people in the spirit of Communist morality, and spiritually regenerate man, it is not possible to build a Communist society."[15]

It is of particular relevance that Ilyichov should posit a necessary connection between the demand for a New Man and the development of the future aims of Communism. What Ilyichov recognized was that the future depended on the growth of the so-called production factor personality. According to Marxism, the Communist society of the future will only be made possible through a high rate of per capita productivity. Such a high rate of productivity, however, could not be obtained by outward norms, coercion or incentives, but only through the efforts of a selfless, conscientious New Man who acts from inner conviction. This is why the change in man is regarded as decisive, a prerequisite for the final change of the structures of society, for example, the abolition of compulsory work.

Likewise, the "withering away of the state" and its reduction to a mere organ of administration (that is, the termination of present dictatorship) could not come about until the New Man had evolved. A minimum of voluntary initiative demands a maximum of direction. Voluntary performance of one's duty and spontaneous, responsible action on the part of renewed persons are the necessary conditions for any final lifting of state coercion. The New Man is the prerequisite of freedom.

Thus, Ilyichov identified the genesis of the New Man as the indispensable precondition for the success of the whole Communist program. At a number of places in his massive speech he made this clear in a pointed fashion. He said that if we fail to generate the New Man who will do the necessary and good spontaneously and in cooperation with his fellow men, we will not be able to realize the Communist vision of a society free of exploitation. The problem of the New Man becomes the fateful question of the future of the Communist movement. It also signals: whoever wishes today to change social structures and conditions will have to face the necessity of changing man tomorrow.

The New Creation in Christianity

The Christian message speaks above all about the history of the realization of God's plan of salvation in the history of humanity. The gospel speaks of the salvation of humanity in terms of justification (that is, in terms of a solution to the problem of human guilt). At the same time, however, Christianity also proclaims the need for an essential change and renewal, a "re-creation" of the person.[16]

As we set out to describe some characteristics of renewed humanity, we reflect especially on those which are relevant to the Marxist concept of the New Man.

The Christian has a Creator. From a Christian perspective, the new person "is being renewed . . . after the image of its creator" (Col. 3:10). As Christians we know of a Creator, a Father who cares for us and sustains us. We are not alone in the universe. We are not independent and autonomous. Our Creator is also our Lord. Karl Marx thoroughly disapproved of the idea of creation. He passionately opted for the idea of the self-development of humanity. For if man had a Creator he would also have a Lord. That concept was to Marx incompatible with human freedom. For Marx, Prometheus, who had said, "I hate all gods," was "the most prominent saint in the philosopher's calendar."[17]

The titanic element of the radical atheist tradition comes to the fore when Marx says that whosoever does not demand to be a creator of the world, recreating the world after his own image, is not worthy of the spirit of man. He will be damned to dream of himself at night, to fall into the production of religious ideas.[18] In opposition to that the Bible quite clearly states that people cannot and will not be renewed out of their own design and strength, but that they are being renewed according to the image of him who created them.

The Christian has a Savior. Christians know of a living

and effective experience of forgiveness. They have experienced and continue to experience in Jesus Christ what Isaiah promised would be the nature of the Messiah: "A bruised reed he will not break, and a dimly burning wick he will not quench" (Is. 42:3).

Marxism, on the other hand, values the revolutionary vision above all else. Individual lives and freedoms may be sacrificed to attain the desired goal. Marxists then find themselves in the same camp with Friedrich Nietzsche, their declared enemy, who said: "What falleth, that shall one also push."[19] Here weakness is a signal for total annihilation. And looking at the limited means available to the revolutionaries for changing humanity, they will soon have to resort to liquidation instead of renewal of those who are not making progress. Isaiah's message and Christ's respective action, however, connote an attitude unheard of in history. The one who received publicans and prostitutes to forgive them and endow them with new life demonstrates the opposite of the philosophy of the natural man who glorifies himself at the expense of others.

The life of the new person in Christianity is based on forgiveness and on an experience of grace and mercy. Only in this way can the old life and its destructive effect be cut off and left behind. The Promethean ideologies, on the other hand, are all merciless. Christ forgives and presents people with a new beginning. Atheist rulers often build up files, carrying the inscription "To Be Preserved Forever," of the weaknesses and shortcomings of their subjects.[20] The Christian knows the secret of forgiveness and that, without forgiveness, new life is impossible.

The Christian has a model. Christians not only find in Christ a remission of sin and guilt and therefore the removal of a past which might otherwise continue to blackmail their efforts to begin anew, but they also have been given an *example* (Rom. 8:29). This is not an ideal toward which people strive out of their own strength. It is an "aim-image," to which they are being made similar in a continuing process. It is Christ himself who is the image of the new being. The new humanity is being created in his image, by a process of sanctification, a process for which Christ himself is the teacher and the initiator. Being a new person does not merely mean interpreting the old life in a new way. **The Christian has a leader.** Paul writes, "The Lord is the Spirit" (2 Cor. 3:17). Jesus sends his Holy Spirit upon his disciples as the Counselor who will remind them of everything that he taught and will teach them what to do in new situations (Jn. 14:26). The new person is not alone and is not quickly perplexed, but has received the mind of Christ and therefore can act according to the intentions of the Lord. The Christian is also being reminded of Christ when studying Scripture describing the Lord's actions while on earth. Christ's disciple is in possession of a sort of "sixth sense," being a child of God, with the privilege of being led by God's Spirit in all that he does or does not do (Rom. 8:14).

The Christian has an assignment. Isaiah 42 speaks of the Messiah who not only forgives and sustains, but who also brings forth justice in an unusual, quiet way. He not only announces the good and the right, but endows us with the power to do it. Christ's commission to the believers is to spread by word and by action the mercy which they have experienced. The new person in Christ proclaims the gospel and serves the neighbor. The Christian wants to see his neighbor also lifted up, soul and body, as he has been uplifted. The Bible speaks of this twofold service of mercy (2 Cor. 5:17-20; Jn. 13). In no uncertain terms, Christ always described his followers as free servants of others (Mt. 20:25-28; Lk. 10:30-37).

Whereas the age-old philosophy of the natural man contrasts self-enjoyment with service to others, and chooses the former, Christ links self-enjoyment with the old nature and chooses service as the earmark of the new. In Matthew 24:45-51, Christ describes two servants engaging in two types of possible action during his physical absence from earth. We might call them the Provider and the Consumer. The Consumer eats and drinks, seeking intoxication and ecstasy, and beating his fellow servants. He consumes his surroundings for his self-enjoyment. The Provider not only avoids destructive behavior, but also seeks to uphold, support and feed his fellow servants in obedience to his commission. It makes the Provider nothing less than a partaker of God's continuing work of sustaining humanity (Ps. 104: 27).

It is deeply disturbing and simultaneously illuminating to find in one and the same chapter, Matthew 14, the two types of servants existing in reality. King Herod ate sumptuously and drank, and he killed John the Baptist, his fellow servant, for a party whim. Jesus felt pity toward the hungry masses and fed five thousand people. Herod is the Consumer and Destroyer; Christ is the true Servant and Provider for humanity.

We need to understand that both attitudes may be realized today in material terms. For example, today we find the Consumer attitude of self-gratification, the philosophy of the affluent society, and its effects on today's towering problems of ecology and the world food crisis. However, this can also be an attitude of mind: using others for building up oneself, one's work and accomplishments. It may even be a religious attitude: expecting others to nurture you spiritually rather than taking responsibility for their spiritual preservation and progress. Consumer or Provider, these are the choices for each individual. But they are also the choices for groups, churches and whole nations.

The Christian has a future and an eternal destiny. "Here we have no lasting city, but we seek the city which is to come" (Heb. 13:14; see also Phil. 3:20). Evangelicalism during the last hundred years has often been rebuked for its otherworldliness. Now perhaps we are well on our way to a completely this-worldly orientation, forgetting our relationship to the world beyond. Thus, some of us are

prone to quote James 5:1-6 on the sins of the rich, but we
stop short of verse 7, thereby leaving out the biblical consequence: "Be patient, therefore, brethren, until the coming of the Lord." We tend to quote only those passages
which we can sell immediately. In this respect I would
warn evangelicals against dropping their traditional concern for the eternal destiny of humanity.

This warning is underlined in a recent article by Mihajlo
Mihajlov, written when he was in jail for the third time (for
seven years) in Yugoslavia because of his nonconformist
articles. In this article he speaks about the "mystical
experience of captivity," by which he means the paradox
that those who save their souls by holding to the truth and
to the voice of their conscience may in the end save both
body and soul, whereas those who compromise their souls
with lies and corruption in order to save their bodies often
lose both.[21] He speaks of how he has experienced a strong
inner power, an invincible authority and an inner certainty which he calls the voice of God. At one point, he says:
"To follow the calling of one's internal voice means to
qualify all of one's deeds of time in relation to eternity."[22]

This is a strong reminder to Christians that we are to live
"under the perspective of eternity" all the days of our
lives. It is almost a forgotten perspective these days. We
make much of the renewed interest in eschatology in the
twentieth century, but in most ethics textbooks today
there is little or no emphasis on our eternal calling as a
discerning motive of action. To find this one has to go as
far back as Calvin who taught that our earthly life is to be
shaped by our desire for life eternal and the promised
vision of God.[23]

Some of us, from a legitimate concern for evangelical
social action, have been party to the one-sided reorienta-
tion of the Christian faith to the immanent. But we can
see that this is a wrong move. A purely this-worldly orientation, for one thing, will never provide sufficient motivation for Christians during persecution and suffering. They

would think that all is lost. We need to remember that our home is in heaven.

On the other hand, it is interesting to note that the Bible does not picture the Christian pilgrimage as one of passivity and mourning. Even to some who were in exile God bid Jeremiah to write: "Seek the welfare of the city where I have sent you into exile, and pray to the LORD on its behalf" (Jer. 29:7). The deportee is to be involved in the welfare of the city and the land, even if it is not his own. He is not determined by the situation, but by God's commission. In acting upon it the Christian will act as salt to the earth and as light to the world, and he or she will be one of the ten just persons for whose sake a city is saved. We need a balanced view, two times one hundred per cent, a full commitment to our eternal calling, and at the same time a full commitment to our God-given task in the preservation and renewal of others through the gospel.

Chapter 9

The Genesis of the New Man in Marxism

he new humanity is envisioned very differently by Christians and by Marxists. Likewise, their means of achieving this new being will differ. We will look first at the attempts to generate the New Man among Marxists.

Program for a New Man

Countries which publicly espouse the teachings of Marx have tried various methods to transform humanity.

In the Soviet Union one may discern different phases of efforts to create the New Man. According to original Marxist theory the turnover of social conditions (the revolution) will bring about a change in human nature. In the USSR this revolution took place in 1917. So at least the leaders of the revolution are depicted as specimens of the New Man. When a British journalist sent a letter to Radio

Moscow asking how the new type of man was to come about, he received a reply written by a well-known Russian Marxist philosopher saying that the New Man had been created in 1917.

This concept, of course, is vulnerable—especially to a Marxist critique!—because it is a kind of abstract dogmatism which has little to do with reality. It reminds one of those theological dogmatists who, in their distance from actual reality, say that Christians have been born again on Golgotha. Regeneration is no concrete event in our own lives. This implies that our new life in Christ is "hidden" in the ways we live today. In Communism as well as in Christianity, such an alibi, pointing to an unprovable event implied in past history which has to be simply believed, produces an academic estrangement from reality which merely gives a new "interpretation" to the same facts of everyday life. A Communist especially must soon hear the verdict of Marx: that the task is not merely to interpret the world and humanity differently, but to change it.

Therefore, the Soviet claim that mankind was remade in the year of the revolution was not satisfying in the long run. So, according to P. Spoerri, the leadership tried to employ Pavlov's conditioning techniques (training people through habituation to produce desirable action, similar to the training of a dog).[1]

A third method was propagated at the important Twenty-Second Congress of the CPUSSR. Here the creation of the New Man through *education*, especially the education of children, was proposed. The coming generation was seen as the solution—the seed of the new humanity.[2] As Khrushchev and others have indicated, it is no use to inoculate old trees with a new twig. One must plant new trees by concentrating on the education of the small children. (This assumes, as the ancient Greeks did, that people will do what is right and good once they have been taught.) Adults are subjected to a process of partial re-education through Party meetings or through their working brigades.

Similar ideas seem to be at work in China. John Roots wrote in the Indian weekly *Himmat:* "Much more than ever in Russia the history of Chinese Communism shows that stress is being laid on re-education and a 'change of heart' as a method which is to be preferred to massive social removals."[3] Roots reports that Chou En-lai, in the days of Yenan before World War 2, had endless discussions on how human nature could be changed. It was almost as though he had a premonition that this might become the central question of our times: how to tame the tiger of human selfishness in all its different forms.

Since then, another method to bring about the New Man has been tried and perhaps abandoned again in China: the creation of permanent revolutionary pressure on people. This so-called cultural revolution, to be applied every fourth or fifth year, threatens people with the possibility that they would be sent to agricultural labor if they lost their revolutionary zeal. This was intended to eliminate the much-feared "revisionism of the second generation," a "revisionism" which tries to reap the fruits of the revolution in bureaucratic comfort rather than continuing the pursuit of lofty ideals at high personal price. So far, the bureaucrat has historically always been the heir of the revolution.

The Elusive Ideal
Both in Party releases and in recent Soviet literature we find abundant evidence of the difficulties facing the attempt to realize these human ideals. It is here that we encounter the evidence of "the power and secret of evil," as one penetrating analysis described it.[4] The revolution could not remove the evil from the hearts of men and women.

There is the problem of lying. During the leadership of Stalin there were many lies, both secret and open—lies of convenience, justified on an ideological basis. The years after Stalin's death have seen an eruption in Russian literature of works expressing humanity's insatiable longing for the unembellished truth: Give us a bitter truth rather than a sweet lie! The novelist David Granin has one of the characters in his novels say: "Truth never creates damage. Nothing can replace the truth."[5] And Solzhenitsyn writes to the Authors' Association: "Nobody can obstruct the ways of truth, and for the progress of truth I am ready to suffer death."[6]

Stalin had in his time issued this slogan to the Party and the administration: "Trust is good, control is better." But his talking about "healthy mistrust as the best foundation of cooperation" is reversed by modern authors in loud protest. Trust between people, they say, is our most valuable, even if our most precarious, possession.[7]

Yet evil makes its appearance not only in lies, but also in every other form of selfishness: laziness, indifference, whitewashing and careerism. One thinks, for example, of Solzhenitsyn's short story entitled "In the Interest of the Cause." There he showed how the splendid fruits of youthful idealism could be taken over by the bureaucracy.

Daniel Granin, in his novel about a physicist, illustrates some of these developments when he describes the "rake's progress of a scientist":

> It is strange. Lagunev was once an able brain in the realm of electrical theory and produced a number of useful things. Then they made him chairman of a committee. He learned to make speeches, and how to destroy others, and so it went on. Works written by other candidates appeared under his name (and then only brochures or interviews like "My impressions of the congress in England"). And now he is trying to get himself elected as a corresponding member of the Academy.[8]

But there are not only those who want to be on top but others who, in order to get advantages for themselves, create through flattery an empire around an influential man while a factory or a whole nation, goes downhill. It is disturbing to read in the "Twenty Letters" of Stalin's daughter Svetlana how the generals of the Secret Service fabricated such a net of lies around her father that in his last years he no longer had contact with the reality in the country.[9]

Perhaps the most shattering realization recently was the recognition that people can no longer be comfortably divided up into good and bad (the bad ones being the reactionaries), but that, as one Russian author writes, "the weeds" are in us ourselves![10] Other authors describe how mistakes made out of love of comfort and selfishness caused people to lose their freedom. The hero in one fictional story suddenly began to understand himself and to ask: "How is it that on the one hand I am fully committed to the struggle for the high-minded ideals of Communism and on the other hand am at times in the grip of quite different passions?"[11]

The Russian writers recognize selfishness and call it "the serpent in the heart" or "the darkness in ourselves."[12] Suddenly the realization dawned that the revolution in the conditions of property had not brought about the birth of an unselfish man. "The weed" goes on growing. There is guilt in all of man's relations—to the community and to other men. Such evil cannot be explained by reason; it can only be conquered by a "mutation of character,"[13] a change in the actual being of humanity.

Besides selfishness and dishonesty, humanity suffers from the evil originating in its own lust for power. More than anyone else the Yugoslav revolutionary Milovan Djilas has characterized this evil in man as twofold: the lust to possess and the lust to rule. Djilas observes a will for power and domination which goes beyond material greed.[14] This lust has not weakened under socialism, but rather increased in its effects because of the availability of instruments of power in the totalitarian state. The result is a soulless bureaucracy which totally regiments life.

Here we see both the power and the powerlessness of an atheist ideology. It actually results in the shriveling of human feeling and the withering of human relationships, instead of the blossoming of life which the revolutionaries promised themselves and others.

This negative development earned the judgment of the young poet Vosnezenski in 1964: "If man goes under in the process, all progress is reactionary."[15]

In the midst of Socialism authors discover that even as the representative of ideas man does not cease to be the slave of his human nature. The nationalization of the means of production has not produced the selfless man. Even without private property man still remains his own best friend. The weakness of the Marxists, one present-day observer sums up, seems to be that they have overlooked the fact that the changing of conditions is a necessary but not a sufficient condition for producing the new humanity.[16]

So there will be many a "battle on the way" to be fought, as the Russian poets put it, before we reach the goal of a new society. We have not yet reached the stage in history where man can be free from the battle between good and evil. On the contrary, we must learn again about good and evil, honesty and conscience.[17]

In this recognition of the failure of the revolution to transform humanity, moral questions are again coming to the fore. This is most strikingly expressed by the natural scientist and author Georgi Vladimov, who at the end of a realistic description of life on a Soviet ice-fishing vessel writes: "The universe possesses no moral sense. And yet it produces man, who cannot understand where he gets the will to do good to others." The problems always remain the same: the moral worth of the person and the way to its realization. There is no escaping this question.[18]

Coping with the Old Man
The battle for the realization of the ideal of Communism

has resulted in a number of conflicts which to me show the impossibility of man's creating the "new type of man." I come to this conclusion in part through a look at the ways in which Communists have reacted to their apparent failure in this area.

The first fatal historical incident which comes to mind in this regard is the suppression of the alleged mutiny of the sailors of Kronstadt in 1921. Lenin ordered the army to eradicate the very men who had helped bring about the revolution of 1917 in the first place. Those men now felt that the "dictatorship of the proletariat" had become "a dictatorship over the proletariat in the name of the proletariat," and they had asked for a larger measure of democracy within the Party.[19] But Lenin had their effort squelched.

A similar, less bloody, but—in the last analysis—just as tragic event for the history of Communism was the occupation of Prague in 1968 which brought to an end the independent development of Socialism in Czechoslovakia. Both cases show the suppression of spontaneity *within* Marxism and the creation of unity through outward, forceful means.

Shortly after the "Prague spring" of 1968 I found myself in conversation with a member of the Czech Communist Party traveling in the West. He said to me, "Until now we have approached the whole problem the wrong way 'round. We have put the cart before the horse. We have motivated the producing workers, the motor of social development, with the stick. Now we must do it differently. We must put the carrot before the nose of the horse which draws the cart." At the moment I replied, "But people are not horses!"

If a dictatorship of a few in the name of the many seemed inconsistent with the ideals of the revolution, so also is talk about coaxing workers with rewards. Both means are inappropriate ways of seeking to bring about a transformation in humanity. The "carrots" offered to workers under the so-called New Economic Policy were material incentives given for improved industrial production. I am referring here to an economic maneuver first tried in the Soviet Union in the desperate years after the first world war, and then applied in eastern European countries after World War 2. Wages were differentiated to an extraordinary degree, and premiums and offers of promotion of individuals or small working units were promised as benefits to those increasing production. Competition, profit of the individual factory, and a free fixing of product prices—all of them elements of capitalism—were reintroduced in the production process for a certain period of time.

These measures indicate that the Communists are employing the weaknesses of the old humanity when in fact they are supposed to be creating the New, selfless Man. By this paradoxical rekindling of egotism on the road to socialism, they water the poisonous plant of self-centeredness which has been declared the root of all evil in human society. To use a comparison much loved in parts of Africa, they are trying to cross the river on the back of the crocodile.

The concern and criticism that this procedure must awaken in the genuine communist has been punctually voiced by the late Ché Guevara when he wrote, "There still remains a long stretch to be covered in the building of the economic base [the level of development which is deemed necessary for the true communist society] and the temptation to follow the beaten paths of material interest as the lever of speedy development is very great." Such temptations include "pursuing the chimera of achieving socialism with the aid of the blunted weapons left to us by capitalism (the commodity as the economic cell, profitability and individual material interest as levers, etc.)." The damage done by this procedure may not be immediately evident. However, the material basis chosen (that is, the material interest of the individual) in the meantime will have "undermined the development of consciousness." If we train people (even temporarily) using the philosophy that they are their own best friends, we create the worst candidates for Communism. Egotism is no logical prerequisite for the creation of the selfless man. Therefore, Guevara concludes, "To build communism, a new man must be created simultaneously with the material base."[20] The good purpose does not sanctify bad means, but bad means destroy the good purpose.

Repression and material incentives—the stick and the carrot—have been the two steps Marxism has taken toward its ideals and two measures which continue up to the present to work against each other.

Transformation through Indoctrination
In addition to the use of "administrative measures" (coercion) and of material incentives, the Soviet Union has also attempted to create the New Man by increasing political education. When Leonid Ilyichov in his programmatic speech spoke of the need for and the qualities of the New Man, he also seemed to imply that failure in attaining this goal was possible. He reported a number of cases where Party functionaries, despite all efforts, were unable to cope with the problem of alcoholism. Some young workers had sent letters to him saying, "It is not that we do not have good intentions. But then some days we are gripped by the wrong spirit; we demolish windows and destroy our workshop. My friend has already been to gaol for this, and I have had to appear before the comrades' court several times. But we can't help it...!" So Ilyichov encouraged his audience to intensify their efforts toward ideological indoctrination of young workers.[21]

At the same time Leonid Ilyichov seems to have encountered the reality of the Christian new man. It is reported (the story has circulated in eastern Europe) that in the sixties Ilyichov, who combines the ideal of the New Man with considerable hostility toward religion, was given the task of producing a survey on why the influence of Christianity in the Soviet Union is on the increase. It is said that his investigation produced the following four reasons:

1. Christians are usually highly trustworthy workers and very often are given positions of high responsibility, such as driving cranes and so forth. Therefore, they gain good reputations among the populace.

2. Christians have solved the problem of alcoholism (a major factor in the setback of industrial production in the Soviet Union) for themselves.

3. Christians maintain peaceful relations in their families and even help toward reconciliation in their neighbors' families when they are on the brink of breakdown. They do more than just talk about peace in conferences and in resolutions.

4. Christians will let no one die without consolation. This may sound strange, but again it is of no small significance in a collectivist society where there is an ongoing public debate on the meaning of the life and death of the individual.

Ilyichov is said to have assured his colleagues that he, along with the administration, would do everything possible to surpass these results of Christian living by intensifying Marxist, atheist instruction. Will he have success? The story came to me with a comment by one of the leaders of the Russian Baptist Church. He confirmed the story. When asked what he thought of the prospects of the Marxist program of indoctrination, he answered, "I am a loyal citizen of my nation. But I do not think that Marxism will be able to achieve the results it is looking for. On the other hand if a person is fully gripped by Christ it will shine forth in everything he does."

The concept of a New Man in Marxism is a splendid ideal, but it will not be realized by human means alone.

Final Evaluation

I believe that the Marxist program of the self-improvement of humanity is bound to fail. I think of two reasons, one based on the Marxist argument itself and the other from a Christian perspective.

First, the deepest reason for the spiritual breakdown of Marxism is a fundamental self-contradiction which lies at its base. This exists in the fact that a materialistic and Darwinist concept of the genesis and development of the world cannot be reconciled with the demand for brotherliness and solidarity.

The aging spokesman of liberal theology in the nineteenth century, David Friedrich Strauss, wrote a book on *The Old and the New Faith* in which he espoused Darwinism but nevertheless asked for an ethos of tolerance and love of neighbor. The clever young philosopher Friedrich Nietzsche exposed this position as sheer nonsense. He pointed out that the material world in its development does not produce or understand the quality of mercy. The result of Darwin's theory of evolution could only be the fight of each person against the other, the rule of the jungle and the survival of the fittest.[22] An evolutionary theory based on competition cannot produce a society where the highest value is love of neighbor.

In the same way Marxism as *materialist socialism* is a paradox, a self-contradiction. It must get entangled in all kinds of theoretical and practical inconsistencies. Its presuppositions do not support its aims.

This tension finds expression in the continuing theoretical struggle between Marxist philosophers and economists over the need for a change in man. Sometimes this even includes debates behind closed doors at Party caucuses over whether the subject should be included in or dropped from platforms for forthcoming public debates. It is considerations of this nature which recently caused the Rumanian Josif Ton, a professor of theology and a widely known preacher, to ask in an open letter addressed to his government: How can a New Man come about when those concerned, especially the young generation, notice the discrepancies between the materialism of the basic philosophy and the lofty ideal, and use the former for their orientation in daily life and practice? Where materialism is presupposed there is no motivation for unselfishness. Materialism remains the chains for the whole project. Professor Ton concluded that socialism, in order to work, needs nothing less than Christianity. It must get rid of atheism.[23]

Where this call is not heeded Marxism finds itself back at the beginning. The problem of the emancipation of humanity from egotism, seen as fundamental by Marxism itself, remains unsolved.

The lack of a deeper motivation for unselfish action also makes Marxist Communism appear as an elaborate, but unfounded idealism. Speaking in theological terms, it demands of man a life of sanctification without the preceding experience of regeneration. Soviet Party literature, which has much to say about the revolution of society, nowhere speaks in concrete terms of the revolution of the individual,[24] although it is the individual of whom a new, selfless way of life is expected. As has already been shown in our comments on methods of suppression and indoctrination, Marxism, theologically speaking, is a kind of *legalism* which expects good fruit from bad trees and seems to assume that exhortation will lead to realization. It is a form of pharisaic religion—the attempt to reach a new life by "works of the law" and without a change of heart first. That did not work in early Judaism, and it will not work in Marxism either. The mere proclamation of the right does not by itself produce its realization.

In Marxism, the problem of motivation has not yet been solved. A change of structures—as can be seen in the revolution of 1917—rarely is more than a change of laws (that is, of demands made on people from the outside). Laws can repress evil, but rarely do they create good. This is due to the negative character of the law. The new laws concerning property which were made after the revolution have not yet changed people's attitude toward property. There is plenty of evidence for this in Soviet newspapers, but also in Ilyichov's speech mentioned above. The abolition of private property does not mean the abolition of the human instinct to acquire private property[25] or of the instinct for increase. The new laws certainly hinder the activity of this instinct, but at the same time they generate a constant struggle of the individual against the law, the continuous attempt to circumvent the law. The law (and this is what the apostle Paul's theology is very clear about) awakens human resistance. Laws alone mean education for corruption. Coercion never changes anyone lastingly and from the roots up. Coercion remains a source of unceasing trouble with the old creature. Of course laws are needed, but beyond that it takes a change of inner motivation.

This point is well made by Paul in Galatians 3:2 when he asks his friends: "Did you receive the Spirit by works of the law, or by hearing with faith?" If they received the Spirit and its predisposition for doing good and for brotherly love from the law, then the law indeed was able to regenerate them. But this it will never do, neither in Christendom nor in Marxism. The law does not change the hearts of men and women. They need the proclamation of a gospel which will bring about a true revolution within them.

Marxism has failed to change the human heart. The popular contemporary writer from Croatia, Miroslav Krleza, has said:

Man does not change in his physical or his moral structures when structures of social relationships are being changed.... Liars continue to speak lies in Socialism. Imposters continue to cheat. Murderers continue to commit murder. And those who stand up for the truth, continue to die for their ideals.... The liberation of man from his wild instincts remains the most disturbing moral and poetical theme of our time.[26]

Chapter 10

The Christian Response: New Birth through Faith

The Marxist pictures the New Man as a person who independently and out of inner conviction does what is good and necessary for the community and who has the capacity for teamwork and the power to reconcile others. This image is absolutely right, and to realize it, an indispensable task.

But when we look at this image, the question of how to realize it arises with renewed urgency. We must not fall into the disillusionment and cynicism which come when people fail in their ideals. For both in the East and the West the New Man is the prerequisite for and the guarantee of freedom. There is no point for us to shake our heads over the battle for a New Man in Soviet Marxism. This is a task which faces all of us. As Georgi Vladimov has said, we cannot avoid it.

We have noted that the history of humanity basically is the story of the struggle between what we call the Consumer and the Provider. Therefore, according to the Christian conception, man with his natural consumer attitudes needs to be changed to become a provider. We have to realize that the prime requirement for the birth of a new humanity is liberation from deep-seated egotism. We cannot simply proclaim the general transformation of society. As Marx said in the beginning, change must take place in the individual and the individual's concrete relationships.

Christianity replaces the futile endeavors—as we are forced to conclude—by Marxists to create the New Man through education and social pressure with the birth of a new person through faith. Christianity also says that change in a person is necessary and possible. However, we say, with the words of the German poet Matthias Claudius, "Man must be improved, and, would I advise, not from the outside."[1] Christian faith speaks of a regeneration of a person from within, of a *new creation*. We will look at this idea in three stages: the start, the road and the power.

The Start
How can such a change in one's way of life become possible? Where would the new motives come from? It is interesting to discover that the confessional writings of the Reformers tackled this very problem of a change in motive. In his "Apology of the Augsburg Confession," Melanchthon writes that where the Holy Spirit, God's gift, comes into the heart and will of a person, he brings with him "new impulses and new works," new motives, a new driving force from within, willingness and creativity that are in consonance with everything needed for the sustainment and development of nature and people.[2]

Before the new person can rise, however, there has to be an experience of *dying* on the part of the old one. The Reformer illustrated this by referring to the story of the prostitute (Lk. 7:37-50) who, coming to Christ, fell at his feet and cried. She lamented her wasted life, the disgrace of which she felt in his presence. "In her tears we recognise her contrition," concludes Melanchthon. The key idea here is *repentance*.

Aleksandr Solzhenitsyn is today looking for this same experience on a national scale. In his press interview in Zürich in 1974 he spoke of the need for an experience of repentance, a wave of cleansing. He demanded that we should stop blaming others and "everyone should combine repentance with the acknowledgment of one's own guilt. This would immediately change the atmosphere."[3]

Put in theological terms this means that the death of the old person and the resurrection of the new one come about in the act of *confession*. You recognize and acknowledge your sin and believe and accept God's mercy upon you. In the presence of Christ one not only discovers one's guilty past but becomes free of it and free for the future. This experience may still be had today.

There is no way to the new being except through the destruction of the old one. The cross comes before the resurrection. That is true for individuals today. Truth comes to power only through conflict. A person is confronted with absolute moral standards and experiences a general re-evaluation of life. The old being dies, and God's pardon brings the new creation to life. The Holy Spirit who creates spontaneity for doing good and acting brotherly is being given to those who repent and pray. Then the new person gives up self-will, leaves the old ways behind and makes restitution where he has harmed others.

The Road: Altered Relationships
This rebirth must also immediately affect human relationships. When a person's life is renewed, change is not limited to the inner life, but will also affect the smallest social unit, the brick of human society: you and your brother. Jesus says in Matthew 5:23-24, "If you are offering your gift at the altar, and there remember that your brother has

something against you, leave your gift there before the altar and go; first be reconciled to your brother, and then come and offer your gift." Being newly created also means being reconciled. Breaking down the walls between us and our neighbors—Jesus calls this even the prerequisite for our further communication with God. Unity comes through change.

When people are changed so much that their motives are transparent to others, then they have become persons others will readily trust. In the political arena recently there has been much talk of the "credibility gap" between politicians and the general electorate. This gap can also be observed in every other human relationship. For Zacchaeus, who held the hated position of tax collector, the credibility gap was closed after he met Jesus (Lk. 19:2-10). He said that he would give half of his wealth to the poor and restore four times any wealth he had acquired through fraud. From now on he was trustworthy.

In this way, using the terminology of the revolutionaries, "liberated pockets" can be established, areas of human life which are liberated from the dominion of selfishness and division. We are thinking of action groups which radiate out into society, bringing about what Lenin described as the selfless initiative of small groups, through whose committed fight a turning in the mood of the masses becomes possible. There are numerous examples of this in the history of Christianity, among them the early Franciscan movement in the thirteenth century and William Wilberforce and the "Clapham Sect" in the nineteenth century.

The future lies with small, spontaneous groups who live by the government of God and effect reconciliation among people in the decisions of everyday life or, as Marx put it, "in their empirical life, their individual work and their individual relationships."

Small groups of renewed men and women who bring about reconciliation are the real renewers of society, people who do not merely invent some cost-saving technical innovations, but are the renewers in the social sphere for whom Soviet philosophers have been searching. For the real problem in society is that the development of human relationships has not kept pace with technological progress.

It may be that national and international politics are of secondary importance when it comes to the development of a truly humane society. Such a society can only begin at a "grassroots" level. However good a government's intentions may be, for instance, toward a neighboring country, if they are not supported by voluntary initiatives which turn public feelings toward reconciliation, these good intentions will come to nothing. In a democracy, government cannot easily make policies without public support, and in the long term a dictatorship cannot do so either.

This is how the renewal of society would be effected: changed individuals would work as groups initiating programs for the welfare of society using the principles of democracy and persuasion until new laws have achieved solid public support and can then be passed. To avoid the labors implied in this is to open the door to dictatorship and to move further away from the the goal of a humane society.

Power for the New Creation

The basis for Marxism is, "Prometheus is the finest saint in the philosopher's calendar." This is one of Marx's very first published sentences. In our context, it means that the new humanity must be created by humanity itself. There is no one else to do it.

Against this the Bible says that people cannot cope with their own guilt, sin and evil. The emancipation of humanity from selfishness must be *received*. It must come from God. We must hear what God has to say to us. God has spoken. From him we find a strength and a wisdom which overcomes human fallibility and makes us new people. On the basis of listening to God we will do good without needing material incentives.

The refusal to listen and lack of openness soon become obstacles to the progress of life and create an impoverished humanity. God's instructions produce spontaneity for good, human sympathy, creative ideas, fellowship and reconciliation. It is therefore necessary to support the vision of a new humanity, but at the same time to show that the power comes from listening to God.

We can learn by looking at how Jesus made his decisions. In John 5:30 we read: "I can do nothing on my own authority; as I hear, I judge ... because I seek not my own will but the will of him who sent me." Jesus' goal, to do the will of God, is so clear and overriding that nothing else finds a place in his life. When he says he can do nothing of himself he means it is no longer one man's will being done, which leads to division, but God's will. That counts most with him. He is so determined that he can say: Of myself I can do nothing. This is not to say that he would remain beneath human possibilities, but go beyond them.

The decisive steps forward in the history of mankind have never come from human wisdom or power. In caring for those entrusted to us we all find how helpless and witless we are. We are like the person who is asked to repair a complicated electronic computer when he hasn't even learned how to repair a flashlight. Human relationships are far too delicate and too complicated for us to be able to mend. We only cause further damage. In view of this Jesus says that he does not handle human relationships at his own discretion. As he hears, so he judges.

As we act likewise, we are not left to our own easily exhausted strength. Once we are free from illusions about our own powers, we can then begin to seek from God the greater strength and persistence needed for the larger tasks. It is a matter of placing ourselves at God's disposal, of being ready to accept his orders and do his works. In short it is a matter of acting out of receiving.

Conclusion

Let us look back on what has been said and decide what it means for our own thinking, perspective and action. I can see its application on three levels: first, for Christianity in general; second, for those Christian groups which are within the evangelical tradition; and finally, for every single person.

Marxism deserves a place of respect within the history of secular humanism for its emphasis on the need for a "new type of man" and a new society. At least as a goal this is more worthy than the programs of self-actualization peddled in the West. Marxists postulate that humanity cannot remain as it is, but must be changed. They do not expect to create the Golden Age using unrenewed humanity as the raw materials.

This indeed holds a challenge for today's Christians. How do we view the present and the future? What prominence do we give to the subject of regeneration and rebirth? Do we believe we can serve humanity purely through ecology and antinuclear campaigns, leaving out the fight for the transformation of persons and their basic motives?

The Bible says that only ten just people could save a city. Either we shall find the creative minority of men and women who, renouncing self, live for the salvation of the world, or we shall have chaos and destruction. The need is for repentance, the human side of God's work of regeneration. In accepting or refusing the new birth through faith, nations decide their fate.

This spells out the responsibility of Christians. Karl Jaspers, the great existentialist philosopher, wrote in his book *The Future of Mankind:*

In today's extremity, the best chance may lie in the churches, insofar as their members still believe . . .[but]

the Church must have a deeper influence, as it has always claimed, on every individual. There its demands must become so serious, so strict, so clear, so unconditional—without adjusting to average frailty and to the evil in men.... In a new earnestness, they [the churches] would repeat the eternal challenge to man: to be changed in his foundations—and in conjunction with his everyday life, with all that men do and think. ... In themselves, the churches would beget the change they are to stimulate in man at large. The human situation, now as ever, demands a rebirth of man....

Biblical religion holds within it the strength of great reason, everybody's inevitable responsibility before Transcendence....

However, if they [the churches] cannot rouse themselves out of their entanglement in worldliness and worldly cunning to an earnest faith in God, they will drift along with the rest, on the road to perdition.[4]

It is moving to hear this non-Christian philosopher nevertheless remind Christendom of its most important task, the concern for the regeneration of humanity. He is right. Churches should consider it their commission to be birth clinics, and the individual Christians midwives of the new humanity. Without such rebirth among men and women, society will continue to decay and nations cannot in the long run live in peace.

But the encounter with Marxism will also have a particular significance for evangelical Christians. Today's situation presents them with dangers and opportunities alike. One of the dangers to evangelicalism results from the fact that it has been mainly individualistic during its last hundred years of history. It is now vulnerable to a sudden swing to the other extreme at a time of pressing social questions. So far evangelicals have had enough conscience to be deeply disturbed by the challenge of today's needs, but they do not have the guidelines necessary to respond biblically to these challenges.

Because of this tradition, there is today some danger of evangelicals falling victim to promising social programs as soon as they go beyond their inherited narrow circles. When secular solutions seem effective against pressing social needs, credulous evangelicals may be taken in. The solutions may be proposed by Marxists or by very different political groups. The postulate of "Food, Clothing and Work for All!" has been realized in Red China today. But it was also realized in the early years of National Socialism.

In such a situation, some evangelicals tend to share the popular opinion that the philosopher's stone has now been found, and they hail whatever maneuver is announced next. Political and theological dilettantism often closes the eyes to the law of revolutions whereby the solidarity and equality propagated early on gives way to power struggles among the leaders. The revolutionary ethos disappears behind a personality cult or intrigue.

Evangelicalism today, as it becomes aware of its social responsibility, must not accommodate itself to the trends of the day, either of the right or of the left. Instead, repentance and conversion are needed so that God is understood and accepted again as the reigning factor in the lives of individuals and society.

Evangelicalism today must flee ideological dependence and formulate a social ethic informed by holy Scripture. Only then will we stop identifying social concern and reform with Marxism. Conservatives have made this identification in order to defame the idea of social change. Progressives have made it by giving a Marxist profile to their social diagnosis and therapy. Both of these are wrong. Faith cannot begin and end with the individual. It must reach out to society, to the world. Likewise, faith cannot simply provide the motivation for actions determined by ideologies hostile to it. Faith and action must be integrated.

Evangelicalism needs to break out of its traditional narrow circles to take responsibility for society, firstly in community affairs. It must "go public," taking with it its central message. This, then, is where today's situation reveals extraordinary opportunities for evangelicals. They have always made the message of the regeneration their main concern. And that is what the world needs. Today's ideological situation cries out for this very message. The gospel has the answers to the questions being asked today. Evangelicals must on no account reduce or give up for the sake of some secular social solution their proclamation of the need for a new birth. Rather, this message is the very key to Christian social reform.

The message we must declare is the message of human regeneration—but including relationships to people and things. This has not always been the content of our message. A friend of mine working among Christian students wrote recently, "My deep concern is the fact that for most of our Christian students faith and conversion seem to be a matter of emotions, but not of a real change in the decisive questions of life. That is the reason for their lack of availability for our task in the universities. Much of their Christianity is indeed an 'opiate,' sometimes even the singing. This will be my main battle—not to be content with anything less than their individually making their lives available to God, including their jobs, friendships, and marriage. 'Here am I, Lord, send Thou me!' "

We must certainly not give up our message and goal of regeneration which is our best heritage. It must be the message of a regeneration not only of the soul or of our moods, but of an inclusive rebirth, a regeneration of "gross weight." The conversion of Zacchaeus must be our guideline, showing how true conversion changes the whole person, including the direction of the cash flow!

Jesus' statement, "Make the tree good, and its fruit good . . . ; for the tree is known by its fruit" (Mt. 12:33) remains true. Social change, reconciliation and welfare are possible but not without the prerequisite of the concrete, personal renewal of people. We are aware of the fact that this renewal cannot be manipulated. It cannot be programmed to undergird wide-flung social reforms. Regeneration takes place only as God decides. These reborn individuals and small groups, however, which come as a gift to humanity when we pray for them, will then act as the salt of the earth and sustain the whole.

Finally, this issue of the "new creation" is already built into every human life. Each one of us is confronted again and again with the question of how life can be renewed. We are forced to ask ourselves: What am I living for? Where do I stand? What have I made of my life?

The new person in each one of us has a history running through our earthly lives—lessons learned, new beginnings, perhaps the abortion of the new creation we should have become, or the birth of the new person, its growth, its training.

For Christians, the encounter with Marxism in its search for the New Man throws out the challenge to become truly new persons who, as Marxism formulates, have left their past behind and who, we would add, make the interests of humanity their own according to the instructions of Jesus. We must each consider for ourselves where we stand in this unfolding story—the story of the new person which we are meant to be.

Notes

Chapter One: The New Appeal of Marxism

[1]*Die Welt* (daily newspaper, Hamburg, Germany), 5 Mar. 1976. Max Hayward has compared Marxism-Leninism with a "dead dinosaur" which "was artificially kept in being" in Russia until Stalin finally stifled it. It was "a dead dogma in which nobody believes." *Religion and the Search for New Ideals in the USSR*, W. C. Fletcher and A. J. Strover, eds. (New York: F. A. Praeger, 1967), pp. 131-32. Perhaps Henry Kissinger was more realistic when he made it his principle "to take seriously the ideological commitment of Soviet leaders." *White House Years* (Boston: Little, Brown, 1979), p. 128.

[2]*Die Welt*, 9 Feb. 1974.

[3]L.c. February 9, 1974: D. Cycon writing under the headline, "The Longing for Faith and Certainty."

[4]At this point I wish to state that Marxism is not merely a doctrine in the field of economics. However, it may be necessary to remind us that even within political economy, Marx, because of the wider range of his concern, did not simply give equality as his ideal. He criticized not only the merely political equality achieved by the French Revolution (see *Karl Marx, Frederick Engels: Collected Works*, vol. III [New York: International Publishers, 1975], p. 163) but also the concept of an "equality of wages" in primitive and "crude Communism" which as a consequence of "the urge to reduce things to a common level" (pp. 294-95) would "disregard talent" and "negate the personality of man in every sphere." "In the higher phase of communist society," which is Marx's goal, "will society be able to inscribe on its banner: From each according to his ability, to each according to his needs!" "Critique of The Gotha Programme 1875," in *Karl Marx, Selected Writings in Sociology and Social Philosophy*, ed. T. B. Bottomore and M. Rubel (Harmondsworth, England: Penguin Books, 1963), p. 263.

[5]See J. Monnerot, *Sociology of Communism*, trans. J. Degras and R. Rees (London: George Allen and Unwin, 1953), pp. 8ff.

[6]Quoted in H. Rolfes, *Der Sinn des Lebens im marxistischen Denken* (Dusseldorf: Patmos, 1971), p. 200.

[7]Ibid., p. 189.

[8]"[Criticism's] essential sentiment is *indignation*, its essential activity is *denunciation*." K. Marx, "A Contribution to the Critique of Hegel's Philosophy of Right: Introduction" in *Karl Marx, Frederick Engels: Collected Works*, vol. III (New York: International Pub., 1975), p. 177; also *Karl Marx: Early Writings*, trans. Rodney Livingstone and Gregor Benton, (Harmondsworth, England: Penguin Books, 1975), p. 246.

[9]Cf. "This *abject materialism, this sin against the holy spirit of the people and humanity.*" K. Marx, "Debates on the Law on Thefts of Wood" (1842) in *Collected Works*, vol. I (1975), p. 262.

Chapter Two: The Challenges of Marxism

[1]*Collected Works*, III, 141; *Early Writings*, p. 206.

[2]*Early Writings*, p. 207; *Collected Works*, III, 142.

[3]"*War on the German conditions! By all means! They are below the level of history, beneath any criticism,* but they are still an object of criticism like the criminal who is below the level of humanity but still an object for the *executioner.*" *Collected Works*, III, 177; *Early Writings*, p. 246.

[4]*Collected Works*, III, 177-78; *Early Writings*, pp. 246-47.

[5]*Collected Works*, III, 176; *Early Writings*, p. 244.

[6]"Theses on Feuerbach" (1845) in *Collected Works*, vol. V (1976), p. 5; *Early Writings*, p. 423.

[7]*The Book of Concord: Confessions of the Evangelical Lutheran Church*, trans. and ed. Theodore G. Tappert, Jaroslav Pelikan et al. (Philadelphia: Fortress, 1959), p. 475.

[8]A. Schlatter, *Rückblick auf meine Lebensarbeit*, 2nd ed. (Stuttgart: Calwer Verlag, 1977), p. 90. Compare his assessment of the evangelical (Protestant) church "which often was great in suffering, in acting however timid and weak." *Luthers Deutung des Römerbriefs*, Beiträge zur Förderung christlicher Theologie 21,7 (Gütersloh: C. Bertelsmann, 1917), p. 60. He also mentions "the cleavage between dogma and ethics which has robbed the German Evangelical Church of its power" in *Die Entstehung der Beiträge zur Förderung christlicher Theologie*, Beiträge zur Förderung christlicher Theologie 25,1 (Gütersloh: C. Bertelsmann, 1920), p. 62.

[9]*Collected Works*, vol. IV (1975), p. 95. *The Holy Family* opens with the words "*real humanism.*"

[10]Ibid., p. 53.

[11]They describe "religious hypocrisy" as that "which takes away from *another man* what he has deserved in respect of me in order to give it to God, and which in general regards everything human in man as alien to him and everything inhuman in him as *really* belonging to him." Ibid., p. 173.

[12]This appears in an autobiographical sketch for the album of the evangelical theology faculty at Münster University in 1927. See "Karl Barth-Rudolf Bultmann, Briefwechsel," in *Karl Barth–Gesamtausgabe*, vol. 1, ed. B. Jaspert (Zurich: TVZ, 1971), p. 307.

[13]I have documented some of these developments in my book, *Atheismus in der Christenheit. Die Unwirklichkeit Gottes in Theologie*

und Kirche, (Atheism within Christendom: The Unreality of God in Today's Theology), vol. I, 2nd ed. (Wuppertal: Aussaat, 1970).

[14]See F. Engels, "Letters from Wuppertal," Collected Works, vol. II (1975), pp. 7ff.

[15]See, for example, M. Machovec, Marxismus und dialektische Theologie. Barth, Bonhoeffer und Hromadka in atheistisch-kommunistischer Sicht (Zurich: TVZ, 1965).

[16]This conception also dominates Marxist psychology, contrary to doctrines in the West: "Soviet psychology has explicitly fostered the theory that consciousness is the highest most specifically human level of development of the psyche. . . . The Soviet conception of consciousness is above all tied to action. The most important function of consciousness, says the Soviet psychologist, is to free man from the constraint of the immediate situation, and to permit him to direct his actions towards goals and tasks beyond that situation. 'The first (characteristic of voluntary movement) is the preliminary consciousness of a goal and the presence of striving for its achievement' (Teplov)." R. A. Bauer, The New Man in Soviet Psychology (Cambridge: Harvard Univ. Press, 1952), p. 132.

[17]Vierteljahreshefte für Zeitgeschichte, 1954, p. 131.

[18]W. Leonhard, Child of the Revolution (London: Collins, 1957), pp. 215-16.

[19]See F. Ewen, Bertolt Brecht: His Life, His Art and His Times (New York: Citadel, 1967), pp. 69, 81ff., 95ff. and Klaus Völker, Bertolt Brecht. Eine Biographie (Munich, 1976), pp. 43ff.

[20]Völker, p. 126.

[21]See the "Nachbemerkung" by Hans Mayer, the translator of the German edition of The Words (Reinbek: Rowohlt, 1968), pp. 146-53.

[22]"Hoderer . . . and the other vigilant selfless ones" in P. Weiss, Exile: A Novel, trans. E. B. Garside, Alastair Hamilton, Christopher Levenson (New York: Delacorte, 1968), p. 134. Later he says, "Hoderer's voice was close to me only when he was already dead," p. 237.

[23]From Weiss's "Ten Working Points of an Author in the Divided World," quoted in H. D. Sander, "Das Ende eines 'dritten Weges' " (The End of a "Third Way"), in Die Welt, 18 Sept. 1965.

[24]Die Gallistl'sche Krankheit (Zurich: Ex Libris, n.d.), p. 126.

[25]Die Aesthetik des Widerstands, vol. I, 2nd ed. (Frankfurt: Suhrkamp, 1975), pp. 136, 267.

[26]Brecht—a Choice of Evils: A Critical Study of the Man, His Works and His Opinions (London: Eyre & Spottiswode, 1959), pp. 133ff.

[27]Weiss, pp. 125-26.

[28]The God Who Failed: Six Studies in Communism (London: Hamish Hamilton, 1950), pp. 25-82.

[29]See Koestler's foreword to Willi Münzenberg: Eine politische Biogra-

phie, by Babette Gross, Schriftenreihe der Vierteljahreshefte für Zeitgeschichte, Nos. 14-15 (Stuttgart: DVA, 1967), p. 11. Cf. the observation made by Nadeshda Mandelstam, widow of Ossip Mandelstam the Christian poet who died in Stalin's concentration camps, concerning the years after the revolution: "Nobody noticed that the end had begun to justify the means, and then, as always, gradually been lost sight of." See her memoirs, *Hope Against Hope* (New York: Atheneum, 1970), p. 168. This wise woman's whole book is a commentary on the degeneration of ideology in Soviet society of the twenties.

[30]The English translation carries the title *The Owl of Minerva*, trans. N. Denny (London: R. Hart-Davis, 1959).

[31]See Gross.

[32]*Early Writings*, p. 354 (1844).

[33]"The meaning of life is the combination of subjective intention with objective necessity, the mediation of the correlation between the individual and the objective total societal process, of individual life with all its richness, and the general process of history. This shows that a meaningful life is possible only as experience of self-assertion by purposeful action." G. Winter as quoted in Rolfes, p. 130 (my translation).

[34]*Early Writings*, p. 352 (1844).

[35]"The structural alterations of society do not get rid of the problem of death, rather the contrary." J. M. Lochman, *Encountering Marx: Bonds and Barriers between Christians and Marxists*, trans. E. H. Robertson (Philadelphia: Fortress, 1977), p. 132.

Chapter Three: Marx and Religion

[1]*Collected Works*, III, 175; *Early Writings*, p. 342.

[2]Compare the atheism present already in Marx's poems of 1837, e.g., "Invocation of One in Despair" and "Human Pride," *Collected Works*, I, 563-64, 584ff. See also the detailed investigation by J. Kadenbach, *Das Religionsverständnis von Karl Marx* (doc. diss.,Würzburg, 1967), (Munich-Paderborn-Vienna: Schöningh, 1970), pp. 37ff. For further documentation of Marx's early atheism "of an extremely militant kind," see David McLellan, *Karl Marx: His Life and Thought* (New York: Harper, 1977), pp. 39, 42, 58.

[3]*Collected Works*, III, 3-129; *Early Writings*, pp. 58-198.

[4]*Collected Works*, III, 272; *Early Writings*, p. 324.

[5]*Collected Works*, III, 28; *Early Writings*, p. 86.

[6]From the preface to his doctoral dissertation of 1841, *Collected Works*, I, 31.

[7]"A being only considers himself independent when he stands on his own feet; and he only stands on his own feet when he owes his exis-

tence to himself. A man who lives by the grace of another regards himself as a dependent being. But I live completely by the grace of another if I owe him not only the maintenance of my life, but if he has, moreover, *created* my life," *Collected Works*, III, 304; *Early Writings*, p. 356. "The question about ... a being above nature and man ... implies the admission of the unreality (Unwesentlichkeit—nonessentiality) of nature and man," *Collected Works*, III, 305-6; *Early Writings*, p. 357.

[8]Compare Bakunin's argument: "If God is, man is a slave; now, man can and must be free; then, God does not exist. . . . A jealous lover of human liberty, and deeming it the absolute condition of all that we admire and respect in humanity, I reverse the phrase of Voltaire, and say, that *if God really existed, it would be necessary to abolish him.*" Michael Bakunin, *Selected Writings*, ed. A. Lehning, trans. Steven Cox and Olive Steves (London: Jonathan Cape, 1973), pp. 125, 128.

[9]With view to Marxist Ernst Bloch, J. M. Lochman states: "The basic principle is to 'de-divinize' (Enttheokratisierung) the Bible. That means: rejection of all elements and themes in which God is presented as 'Lord over all.' " Lochman, p. 100. It is this attitude of Marxism which makes Marxism and Christianity incompatible. David Lyon, in his informative new book *Karl Marx: A Christian Appreciation of His Life and Thought* (Tring, England: Lion Publishing, 1979) comes to the same conclusion: "However much Christians have to learn from Marx, there can be no synthesis of the two world-views" (p. 189). Cf. also Dale Vree, *On Synthesizing Christianity and Marxism* (New York: Wiley-InterScience, 1976).

[10]"Religion, at least the Christian, is the relation of man to himself, or more correctly to his own nature (*i.e.*, his subjective nature); but a relation to it, viewed as a nature (Wesen—being) apart from his own. The divine being is nothing else than the human being, or, rather, the human nature purified, freed from the limits of the individual man, made objective—*i.e.*, contemplated and revered as another, a distinct being. All the attributes of the divine nature are, therefore, attributes of the human nature." Ludwig Feuerbach, *The Essence of Christianity*, trans. G. Eliot (New York: Harper Torchbooks, 1957), p. 14.

[11]"Full well I know the earthly round of men,
And what's beyond is barred from human ken;
Fool, fool is he who blinks at clouds on high,
Inventing his own image in the sky.
Let him look round, feet planted firm on earth:
This world will not be mute to him of worth,"
—Goethe's prophecy of the mentality of the upcoming industrial era. *Faust*, part 2, trans. Philip Wayne (Harmondsworth, England: Penguin, 1959), p. 265.

[12]*Ausgewählte Briefe von und an Ludwig Feuerbach* (Selected Letters), ed. W. Bolin (Leipzig, 1904), vol 1, p. 293.

[13]From his "Thoughts on Death and Immortality. Stanzas on Death" (1830):
"Your God is nothing but yourself,
But neatly polished and adorned.
And 'tis this separated I which
sets up itself as God for self.
An object makes itself the I,
That is the theme of the comedy."
Ludwig Feuerbach, *Sämtliche Werke*, vol. III, 3rd ed. (Leipzig: Wigand, 1876), p. 107 (my translation).

[14]Compare the second chapter of Feuerbach's *The Essence of Christianity*, pp. 12ff., 27-32. See also R. Lorenz, "Zum Ursprung der Religionstheorie Ludwig Feuerbachs," *Evangelische Theologie*, 17(1957), pp. 171-88. Lorenz points to medieval mysticism as the source, but does not speak of its "positive" and "negative" ways, common since Pseudo-Dionysius the Areopagite, which are the true object of Feuerbach's critical method.

[15]"Participated life is alone true, self-satisfying, divine life—this simple thought . . . is the secret, the supernatural mystery of the Trinity." Ibid., p. 67.

[16]Compare my doctoral dissertation, *Leiblichkeit und Gesellschaft. Studien zur Religionskritik und Anthropologie im Frühwerk von Ludwig Feuerbach und Karl Marx* (Gottingen: Vandenhoeck, 1961), pp. 69ff.

[17]Frederick Engels, "Ludwig Feuerbach and the End of Classical German Philosophy" (1886) in *Marx-Engels, On Religion* (Moscow: Progress, 1975), p. 197. Engels continued, "How enthusiastically Marx greeted the new conception and how much—in spite of all critical reservation—he was influenced by it, one may read in *The Holy Family*." See also Engels's own rendering of Feuerbach's theory in 1844: "Religion by its very essence drains man and nature of substance, and transfers this substance to the phantom of an otherworldly God. . . . Religion represents man's action of making himself hollow (Die Religion ist der Akt der Selbstaushöhlung des Menschen)." "The Condition of England. *Past and Presence* by Carlyle," *Collected Works*, III, 461-62.

[18]"Feuerbach . . . was the first to complete the *criticism of religion* by sketching in a grand and masterly manner the *basic features* of the *criticism of Hegel's speculation* and hence *of all metaphysics*." *The Holy Family* in *Collected Works*, IV, 139.

[19]"The task of history, therefore, once the world beyond the truth has disappeared, is to establish the truth of this world." *Collected Works*,

III, 176; *Early Writings*, p. 244.

[20]"Religion is... the *fantastic realisation* of the human essence because the human essence has no true reality." *Collected Works*, III, 175; *Early Writings*, p. 244.

[21]Ibid.

[22]See the excursus on the expression *opium of the people* in H. Gollwitzer, *The Christian Faith and The Marxist Criticism of Religion*, trans. D. Cairns (Edinburgh: Saint Andrews Press, 1970), pp. 15-21; and E. Benz, "Hegels Religionsphilosophie und die Linkshegelianer. Zur Kritik des Religionsbegriffes von Karl Marx," *Zeitschrift für Religions-und Geistesgeschichte*, 7 (1955), pp. 247-70.

[23]"The criticism of religion disillusions man to make him think and act and shape his reality like a man who has been disillusioned and has come to reason, so that he will revolve round himself and therefore round his true sun." *Collected Works*, III, 176; *Early Writings*, p. 244.

[24]Marx and Engels name Feuerbach "the gnostic" in "The German Ideology" (1846). *Collected Works*, V, 117. Feuerbach remains a "theorist and philosopher" (p. 58) whereas "in reality and for the *practical* materialist, i.e., the *communist*, it is a question of revolutionizing the existing world, of practically coming to grips with and changing the things found in existence" (pp. 38-39).

[25]*Early Writings*, p. 244; *Collected Works*, III, 175.

[26]In Feuerbach's philosophy "the earthly world ... appears merely as a *phrase.*" *Collected Works*, V, 236. Marx and Engels reproach Feuerbach for positing " 'man' instead of 'real historical man.' " *Collected Works*, V, 39. Engels in a letter to Marx in 1846 comments similarly on Feuerbach's essay "The Essence of Religion": "Lengthy rubbish against teleology. Copy of the old materialists. . . . One doesn't hear anything about the historical development of the different religions." *Karl Marx–Friedrich Engels, Briefwechsel, Marx-Engels-Gesamt-Ausgabe*, Abt. 1, vol. III (Berlin: Marx-Engels-Verlag, 1929), pp. 46-47 (my translation). Later, Engels said about Feuerbach, "To him history is altogether an uncanny domain in which he feels ill at ease." *On Religion*, p. 213. Against this, in 1844 Engels consciously announced: "We claim to the meaning (Inhalt) of history." *Collected Works*, III, 464. Cf. Nicholas Lobkowicz, *Theory and Practice: History of a Concept from Aristotle to Marx* (Notre Dame: University Press, 1967), pp. 255-57.

[27]From the minutes of the Communist Workers' Educational Association meetings in London (October 1845), *Marx-Engels-Gesamt-Ausgabe*, Abt. 1, vol. VI, pp. 639-40; compare W. Bienert, *Der überholte Marx. Seine Religionskritik und Weltanschauung kritisch untersucht* (Stuttgart: Evangelisches Verlagswerk, 1974), pp. 129-30.

[28]Marx and Engels censor those who "regard religion as *causa sui*" (its

own cause) "instead of explaining it from the empirical conditions and showing how definite relations (Verhältnisse) of industry and intercourse (Verkehr) are necessarily connected with a definite form of society, hence, with a definite form of state and hence with a definite form of religious consciousness." *Collected Works*, V, 154. In his *Capital*, vol. 1, Marx observed similarly: "Every history of religion . . . , that fails to take account of this material basis, is uncritical. It is, in reality, much easier to discover by analysis the earthly core of the misty creations of religion, than, conversely, it is, to *develop* from the actual relations of life (aus den wirklichen Lebensverhältnissen) the corresponding celestial forms of those relations. The latter method is the only materialistic, and therefore the only scientific one." Consequently, Marx criticizes "the weak point in the abstract materialism of natural science, . . . that excludes history and its process." *On Religion*, p. 119. Engels finally applies this criticism to earlier attempts of unhistorical analyses of Christianity: "A religion that brought the Roman world empire under subjection and dominated by far the larger part of civilized humanity for 1,800 years cannot be disposed of merely by declaring it to be nonsense gleaned together by frauds. One cannot dispose of it before one succeeds in explaining its origin and its development from the historical conditions under which it arose and reached its dominating position. This applies to Christianity. The question to be solved, then, is how it came about that the popular masses in the Roman Empire . . . preferred this nonsense—which was preached, into the bargain, by slaves and oppressed—to all other religions." *On Religion*, p. 171.

[29]"In fact, if we may call Philo the doctrinal father of Christianity, Seneca was her uncle. Whole passages in the New Testament seem almost literally copied from his works." *On Religion*, p. 182. Compare where Engels gives this, with very similar words, as Bruno Bauer's view (pp. 71-72).

Chapter Four: The Legitimacy and Limit of the Marxist Critique

[1]*Sämtliche Werke*, vol. I (Leipzig: Wigand, 1846), pp. 259-325. Further, compare his "Merkwürdige Äusserungen Luthers nebst Glossen" (Noteworthy Utterances of Luther with Comments), ibid., pp. 334-41.

[2]"The *Whence* of our receptive and active existence, as implied in this self-consciousness, is to be designated by the word 'God,' and . . . this is for us the really original signification of that word. . . . So that in the first instance God signifies for us simply that which is the co-determinant in this feeling and to which we trace our being in such a state (unser Sosein zurückschieben)," Schleiermacher, *The Christian*

Faith, ed. H. R. Mackintosh and J. S. Stewart (Edinburgh: T. & T. Clark, 1960), pp. 16-17.

[3]Only "at the present time" such a procedure would be appropriate because of the lack of any historical correlation, see Schleiermacher, pp. 125-26 and his second epistle (Sendschreiben) to Lücke.

[4]Cf. M. Kähler, Geschichte der protestantischen Dogmatik im 19. Jahrhundert, Theologische Bücherei, 16, (Munich: Chr. Kaiser, 1962), pp. 119ff.; and H. Hermelink, Das Christentum in der Menschheitsgeschichte von der Französischen Revolution bis zur Gegenwart, vol. I (Stuttgart and Tubingen: J. B. Metzler/R. Wunderlich, 1951), pp. 412-13.

[5]Johann Christian Konrad von Hofmann in his Scripture Proof, vol. I, p. 10; cf. Kähler, pp. 212ff.

[6]"Therefore ... when the question is raised of how any speaking of God can be possible, the answer must be, it is only possible as talk of ourselves." Faith and Understanding, vol. I, ed. R. W. Funk, trans. L. P. Smith (London: SCM, 1969), p. 61, see also p. 55.

[7]See my Atheismus in der Christenheit, I, 34ff.

[8]See H. Braun, "Die Problematik einer Theologie des Neuen Testaments," in his Gesammelte Studien zum Neuen Testament und seiner Umwelt (Tubingen: J. C. B. Mohr, 1962), pp. 324-41. An in-depth discussion of this, with a view to Marxism throughout, is offered by H. Gollwitzer, The Existence of God as Confessed by Faith, trans. J. W. Leitch (London: SCM, 1965), see pp. 81ff.

[9]For a more detailed study, cf. my Atheismus in der Christenheit, I, 82-89.

[10]The famous-infamous phrase, "A truly penetrating Christian judgment on the nineteenth century, instead of crossing itself with horror at the idea, should regard the asking of just this question so pointedly as one of the few wholly satisfactory achievements of the period" is found in Barth's Theology and Church: Shorter Writings 1920-1928, trans. L. P. Smith (New York: Harper, 1962), p. 213.

[11]Compare the division of "the existence of a Jesus of Nazareth, for example, which can of course (allenfalls—perhaps!) be discovered historically" from that reality with which "the Word became flesh," in Barth's correspondence with Adolf von Harnack in 1923. See M. Rumscheidt, Revelation and Theology: An Analysis of the Barth-Harnack Correspondence of 1923 (Cambridge: University Press, 1972), pp. 19-53 (quotations from p. 44).

[12]See the preparatory notebooks to the lost appendix from Marx's doctoral dissertation (Collected Works, I, 74-76, 102-05, 448ff.). For a discussion compare my dissertation Leiblichkeit und Gesellschaft, pp. 115ff.

[13]Marx says, for example, "Only under the dominance of Christianity,

which makes *all* national, natural, moral, and theoretical conditions *extrinsic* to man, could civil society . . . sever all the species-ties of man, put egotism . . . in the place of those species-ties, and dissolve the human world into a world of atomic individuals who are inimically opposed to one another." *Collected Works,* III, 173; *Early Writings,* p. 24.

[14]"Do not demand from non-believers which do not, as you do, look up with one eye to the heavenly Beyond, and with the other one down to earth, but concentrate both eyes on *one* point, that they should be cross-eyed like you." Ludwig Feuerbach, *Sämtliche Werke,* I, 107 (my translation).

[15]On Christ's double commandment of love, Matthew 22:37-39, which seems to deny this allegation, Feuerbach argues: "But how can the second commandment be equal to the first if that already demands my whole heart and all my strength? What of my heart is left over for man if I am to love God with all my heart?" *Sämtliche Werke,* II (1846), 406 (my translation).

[16]See D. Soelle's essay "Gibt es ein atheistisches Christentum?" (Is There a Christian Atheism?), *Merkur,* 23 (1969), No. 249, pp. 39-40.

[17]Scholarship "demands from us perception which is the source of all thinking." Adolf Schlatter, *Erlebtes* (Berlin: Furche, 1924), p. 80. Compare to this the famous dictum of J. T. Beck the Biblicist of the nineteenth century, which Schlatter loved to cite: "The eye of the wise man sees what is there, but the brain of the conceited composes hypotheses." *Ein Lehrer der Kirche. Worte des Gedenkens an D. Adolf Schlatter. 1852-1938* (Stuttgart: Calwer Verlag, 1938), p. 38 (my translation).

[18]See A. Deissmann, *Light from the Ancient East,* trans. L. R. M. Strachen (London: Hodder, n.d.), p. 155.

[19]Letter of Barnabas, 19, 5.

[20]On Religion, p. 258.

[21]On Religion, pp. 173, 181, 186, 282-83, 299. "Even the historical existence of a Jesus Christ can be questioned" (p. 171). "*Christianity has no history whatever*" (*Collected Works,* V, 154).

[22]"The legend that Christianity arose ready and complete out of Judaism and, starting from Palestine, conquered the world with its dogma and its morals already defined in the main, has been untenable since Bruno Bauer." Engels speaks of the "enormous influence which the Philonic school of Alexandria and Greco-Roman vulgar philosophy—Platonic and mainly Stoic—had on Christianity. . . . Bruno Bauer . . . laid the foundation of the proof that Christianity was not imported from the outside—from Judea—into the Romano-Greek world and imposed on it, but that, at least in its world-religion form, it is that world's own product." *On Religion,* pp. 281-82

(1894-95). Engels expressed hope that further insights might be gained by future discoveries "above all in Egypt" (p. 282).

[23]"Christianity, like every great revolutionary movement, was made by the masses. It arose in Palestine, in a manner utterly unknown to us, at a time when new sects, new religions, new prophets arose by the hundred. It is, in fact, a mere average (eine Durchschnittserscheinung)." Marx-Engels, On Religion, p. 181 (1883).

[24]"Ludwig Feuerbach and the End of Classical German Philosophy" (1886), Marx-Engels, On Religion, p. 230.

[25]W. I. Lenin, On Religion, 3rd ed. (Moscow: Progress, 1969), pp. 70-71.

[26]Albert Schweitzer, Geschichte der Leben-Jesu-Forschung (The Quest of the Historical Jesus), Preface to the 6th edition (Tubingen: J. C. B. Mohr, 1951), pp. XIIIff. (not in the English editions—my translation).

[27]The words of Engels found for Feuerbach's theory of morals might also be applied to his theory of religion: "It is designed to suit all periods, all peoples and all conditions, and precisely for that reason it is never and nowhere applicable." Marx-Engels, On Religion, p. 215. Also see my Leiblichkeit und Gesellschaft, p. 43.

[28]Ibid., p. 70.

[29]Compare the foreword to his dissertation of 1841: "If a critique of Plutarch's polemic against Epicurus's theology has been added as an appendix, this is because this polemic is by no means isolated, but rather representative of an espèce, in that it most strikingly represents in itself the relation of the theologising intellect to philosophy" (Collected Works, I, 30).

[30]For instance, he uses "the spurious writings of S. Bernard." Obviously Feuerbach found the sources for his view of the "essence of Christianity" less in the Bible than in rather diverse writings of the early Church, especially the Middle Ages, and in the writings of Luther.

[31]Compare H. G. Koch, Abschaffung Gottes (Stuttgart, 1961), pp. 91ff.

[32]Compare Gaudium et Spes, the Pastoral Constitution on "The Church in the Modern World" of the Second Vatican Council: "The remedy which must be applied to atheism, however, is to be sought in a proper presentation of the Church's teaching as well as in the integral life of the Church and her members. For it is the function of the Church, led by the Holy Spirit who renews and purifies her ceaselessly, to make God the Father and His Incarnate Son present and in a sense visible." The Documents of Vatican II, ed. W. M. Abbott, S.J. (New York: America-Association Press, 1966), p. 219.

Chapter Five: The Ethics of Marx

[1]Lenin agrees with Sombart's contention that "there isn't a single

grain of ethics in the whole of Marxism, from start to finish." Marxism, concerning theory subjected the "ethical standpoint" to the principle of causality, concerning practice everything was beamed at the class struggle. W. I. Lenin, *Ueber kommunistische Moral* (On Communist Morality) (East Berlin: Dietz, 1965), my translation, pp. 17-18.

[2]Vernon Venable, *Human Nature: The Marxian View* (London: Dobson, 1946).

[3]Helmut Thielicke, *Theologische Ethik* II, 1 (Tubingen: J. C. B. Mohr, 1959), pp. 25ff.

[4]Martin Buber, *Sehertum, Anfang und Ausgang* (Cologne and Olten, 1955), quotations pp. 59, 69. Compare Buber, *The Prophetic Faith*, trans. C. Witton-Davies (New York: Macmillan, 1949), pp. 103ff., 175, 178.

[5]Wilhelm Herrmann, *Ethik*, 5th ed. (Tubingen: J. C. B. Mohr, 1913), pp. 75ff.

[6]Helmut Gollwitzer, *Zum Verständnis des Menschen beim jungen Marx* (On the concept of Man in early Marx), Festschrift G. Dehn, ed. W. Schneemelcher (Neukirchen: Erziehungsverein, 1955), pp. 183-203, esp. pp. 201-02.

[7]"The only writings since Hegel's *Phänomenologie* and *Logik* to contain a real theoretical revolution," Marx in the preface to his economic and philosophical manuscripts of 1844 *(Collected Works,* III, 232; *Early Writings,* p. 281).

[8]"But the essence of man is no abstraction inherent in each single individual. In its reality it is the ensemble of the social relations." Marx states that Feuerbach, because of his approach, is "obliged to abstract from the historical process" (Thesis Six on Feuerbach [1845], *Collected Works,* V, 4; *Early Writings,* p. 423). Engels renders the same view when in his monograph on Feuerbach he writes, "But from the abstract man of Feuerbach one arrives at real living men only when one considers them as participants in history" *(Marx-Engels, On Religion,* p. 216).

[9]Rolf Dahrendorf, *Marx in Perspektive. Die Idee des Gerechten im Denken von Karl Marx,* 2nd ed. (Hannover, 1971). Cf. also David McLellan, *Marx* (Glasgow: Fontana/Collins, 1975), pp. 43, 59.

[10]*Collected Works,* III, 176; *Early Writings,* p. 244.

[11]*Collected Works,* III, 178; *Early Writings,* p. 247.

[12]*Collected Works,* III, 182; *Early Writings,* p. 251.

[13]Marx had early a vivid consciousness of "the present situation," even with a distinction made between the movements of the "hour-hand" and the "minute-hand" of the clock of history (in a letter to A. Ruge, July 9, 1842, *Collected Works,* I, 391) and of what was to be done according to "a definite plan of operations" (in a letter to D. Oppen-

heim, August 1842, (*Collected Works*, I, 392). Compare the same sentiment in the letters written to Marx by his close friend, Bruno Bauer (Karl Marx-Friedrich Engels, *Historisch-Kritische Gesamt-Ausgabe*, ed. by D. Rjazanov, 1.Abt., Bd.1, 2.Halbbd. [Berlin: Marx-Engels-Verlag, 1929], p. 234 [1839], p. 240 [1840], pp. 249, 252 [1841]).

Chapter Six: The Ethics of Lenin

[1]John Keep in L. B. Schapiro and P. Reddaway, eds., *Lenin: The Man, the Theorist, the Leader; a Reappraisal* (New York: F. A. Praeger, 1967), p. 147.

[2]N. K. Krupskaya, *Reminiscences of Lenin*, trans. Bernard Isaacs (New York: International Publishers, 1975), pp. 11-12. The paradox in Lenin's view can clearly be seen in his pronouncement about the hoped-for conversion of a national into a civil war: "We must *allow* this moment to ripen, we must systematically 'force it to ripen' ... " (ibid., p. 294, italics mine).

[3]"The first of these rules is that unswerving dedication to the final aim must be combined with extreme flexibility in the choice of means" (J. Keep, p. 142). Aim-consciousness as a prominent trait in Lenin's character is also witnessed to by many of his contemporaries. See W. Gautschi, *Lenin als Emigrant in der Schweiz* (Zurich: Ex Libris, 1975), pp. 80ff.

[4]Quoted in A. V. Thiesen, *Lenins politische Ethik nach den Prinzipien seiner politischen Doktrin* (Lenin's political ethics according to the principles of his political doctrine) (Munich and Salzburg: A. Pustet, 1965), pp. 212-13 (my translation).

[5]Quoted in Thiesen, p. 97. Regarding the implementation of these views, Lenin's style of unyielding leadership and the consequent splittings in the Party, see L. Schapiro, *The Communist Party of the Soviet Union* (New York: Random House, 1960), pp. 24ff.

[6]Lenin, *Ueber kommunistische Moral*, pp. 226, 228.

[7]Quoted in Thiesen, p. 130.

[8]Lenin, *Ueber kommunistische Moral*, pp. 153-54.
Concerning the Leninist theory of compromise, see Keep, pp. 135ff

[9]Lenin, *Ueber kommunistische Moral*, p. 246.

[10]Cf. the quotations in Thiesen, pp. 84, 80.

[11]Lenin, *Ueber kommunistische Moral*, p. 146.

[12]Ibid., p. 131.

[13]Ibid., p. 132.

[14]Ibid., p. 147.

[15]Compare, for example, I. Rüttenauer, *A. S. Makarenko. Ein Erzieher und Schriftsteller in der Sowjetgesellschaft* (Freiburg: Herder, 1965).

[16]Cf. Richard T. De George in *Studies in Soviet Thought*, vol. III, ed. J. Bochenski (Fribourg, 1963), pp. 83-103, 121-33.

[17]A. F. Schischkin, *Grundlagen der marxistischen Ethik*, 2nd ed., ed. R. Miller (East Berlin: Dietz, 1965), pp. 445-55.

[18]From Clara Zetkin's reminiscences of Lenin in Lenin, *Ueber kommunistische Moral*, p. 282.

[19]Ibid.

[20]Lenin, *Ueber kommunistische Moral*, pp. 281-82. Compare also Lenin's letter to Inès Armand, Jan. 17, 1915, where he rejects the demand for "free love" as a bourgeois demand (ibid., p. 117).

[21]Lenin, *Ueber kommunistische Moral*, p. 37.

[22]Quoted in Thiesen, p. 99. Compare Lenin, *Ueber kommunistische Moral*, p. 99: "The concerns of the cause must be set higher than any personal or group relationship."

[23]"We intend to publish a booklet describing the lives of those workers" (i.e., those who had died during the insurrection of 1905). "Such a book will be the best reading material for young workers who will learn from it how every class-conscious worker must live and act" (Lenin, *Ueber kommunistische Moral*, p. 98).

[24]Ibid., p. 94.

[25]"An unending fascination radiated from Wladimir Iljitsch as a person. His contemporaries who were fortunate to know Iljitsch more closely, rightly point out that the characteristics of his personality represent the prototype of the man of the future communist society. ... He was a true leader of the new humanity" (From the official Lenin biography of the East Berlin Socialist Party publishers, rpt. in Lenin, *Ueber kommunistische Moral*, p. 258). "Without vanity, without personal ambition he is already the 'new man' postulated by Marx." J. Marabini, *Lenin. Organisator der russischen Revolution* (Wiesbaden: Rheinische Verlags-Anstalt, n.d.), my translation, p. 54.

[26]Cf. Krupskaya, pp. 18ff.

[27]Ibid., pp. 27-28.

[28]Ibid., p. 41.

[29]Ibid., p. 61.

[30]Cf. ibid., pp. 77ff.; and the map "Distribution of 'Iskra' in Marabini," pp. 152-53.

[31]Krupskaya, p. 65.

[32]Ibid., p. 103.

[33]Ibid., pp. 127-28.

Chapter Seven: The Challenge to Christian Ethics

[1]According to Adolf Schlatter (*Die christliche Ethik* [Christian

Ethics], 3rd ed. [Stuttgart: Calwer Verlag, 1929], p. 260, n.1), this passage represents "the rule of apostolic work."

[2]In his book *Atheismus in Christentum* (Frankfurt: Suhrkamp, 1968), Ernst Bloch, the shrewd Marxist, postulates not the demythologization, but the detheocratization of the Bible, to the advantage of what he calls the "religion" of humanist utopianism (pp. 110-11).

[3]K. Barth, *Church Dogmatics*, vol. IV: The Doctrine of Reconciliation, pt. 4 (fragment), trans. and ed. G. W. Bromiley (Edinburgh: T. & T. Clark, 1969).

[4]K. Barth, *Church Dogmatics*, vol. III: The Doctrine of Creation, pt. 4, ed. G. W. Bromiley, trans. A. T. Mackay et al. (Edinburgh: T. & T. Clark, 1961), p. 645.

[5]P. Lehmann, *Ethics in a Christian Context* (New York: Harper & Row, 1963).

[6]Cf. G. Wingren, *Luther on Vocation*, trans. C. R. Rasmussen (Philadelphia: Muhlenberg Press, 1957), p. 228.

[7]See, for example, Martin Luther's *Small Catechism in Contemporary English* (Minneapolis: Augsburg, 1963).

[8]Cf. Joseph Fletcher, *Situation Ethics: The New Morality* (London: SCM, 1966); John A. T. Robinson, *Christian Morals Today* (Philadelphia: Westminster, 1964).

[9]See the critique of the "new morality" in my book *Gott im Exil? Zur Kritik der 'neuen Moral'* (Wuppertal: Aussaat, 1975).

[10]See my essay "Revolution of Ethics and Ethics of Revolution" in *International Reformed Bulletin*, Nos. 44-45, Winter/Spring 1971, pp. 52-72, esp. pp. 63-64.

[11]Bockmuehl, *Gott im Exil?*, pp. 179ff.

[12]Cf. H. D. Wendland, *Schriftgebundenheit und Geistesleitung in der urchristlichen Mission* (The original Christian mission: bound by Scripture and led by the Spirit), Jahrbuch für die deutsche evangelische Heidenmission, ed. W. Freytag (Hamburg, 1939), pp. 13-19.

[13]W. Krusche, *Gottes Wege führen weiter* (God's Ways Lead On), Theologische Beiträge, 8 (1977), p. 204 (my translation).

[14]Lenin laid down this principle in *On Religion*, pp. 24-25. For the West, cf. Peter Hebblethwaite, *The Christian-Marxist Dialogue: Beginnings, Present Status, and Beyond* (New York: Paulist Press, 1977), pp. 69ff. on some "Christians for Socialism": As far as content goes, there is no specific contribution made by Christians toward the alliance; "the specifically Christian dimension is found in the motivations provided by faith and hope" (p. 69). On the ensuing loss of Christian identity, cf. Carl Henry, *God, Revelation and Authority*, vol. IV (Waco, Tex.: Word, 1979), pp. 554-77.

[15]Concerning Spain see the considerations of P. Weiss, *Aesthetik des Widerstands*, vol. I, pp. 228ff.; concerning France and Yugoslavia

see Franz Borkenau, *European Communism* (New York: Harper and Brothers, 1953), pp. 315ff, 365ff.

[16]Cf. O. Cullmann, *Jesus and the Revolutionaries*, trans. G. Putnam (New York: Harper & Row, 1970), pp. 58-59.

Chapter Eight: The New Man in Marxism and Christianity

[1]*Collected Works*, III, 164ff.; *Early Writings*, p. 230ff.

[2]Karl Marx-Friedrich Engels, *Historisch-Kritische Gesamt-Ausgabe*, ed. D. Rjazanov, 1. Abt., Bd. I, 1. Halbbd. (Frankfort: Marx-Engels Archiv Verlags gesellschaft, 1927), p. 571. Cf. the words of the Russian revolutionary poet of the nineteenth century, Aleksandr Herzen, as quoted in M. Mihajlov, *Moscow Summer* (New York: Farrar, Straus, and Giroux, 1965), p. 145: "It is not enough to smash the Bastille into pebbles in order to make out of confused prisoners free men."

[3]*Collected Works*, III, 168; *Early Writings*, p. 234.

[4]*Early Writings*, p. 234; *Collected Works*, III, 167-68.

[5]Marx and Engels in "The German Ideology" (*Collected Works*, V, 54). See also Marx's Thesis 3 concerning Feuerbach: "The materialist doctrine concerning the changing of circumstances and upbringing forgets that circumstances are changed by men and that it is essential to educate the educator himself" (*Collected Works*, V, 4; *Early Writings*, p. 422). Cf. my essay "Theorie und Praxis, Änderung des Menschen und Änderung der Strukturen" (Theory and Practice, Change of Man and Change of Structures) in Bockmuehl, *Glauben und Handeln*, *Beiträge zur Begründung evangelischer Ethik* (Giessen and Basel: Brunnen, 1975), pp. 104ff.

[6]Lenin, *Ueber kommunistische Moral*, p. 158.

[7]Ibid., p. 186.

[8]Ibid., p. 186-87.

[9]W. Suchomlinski, *Ueber die Erziehung des kommunistischen Menschen* (The Education of Communist Man), (East Berlin: Volk und Wissen, 1965), pp. 18-19, 23 (my translation). Cf. V. Sukhomlinsky, *On Education*, trans. K. Judelson (Moscow: Progress, 1977), esp. pp. 287ff. on the moral education of children.

[10]Suchomlinski, pp. 28, 30-31, 34.

[11]As quoted by S. Müller-Markus in *Basler Nachrichten*, 3 Aug. 1966.

[12]As quoted in Erwin Hinz, *Die Geburt des neuen Menschen. Tendenzen in der modernen sowjetischen Literatur* (The Birth of the New Man. Trends in modern Soviet Literature, my translation) (Frankfurt: Stimme-Verlag, 1966), p. 37.

[13]Ibid., p. 50.

[14]Translated from *Programm und Statut der KPdSU* (Program and Statutes of the CPUSSR) (East Berlin: Dietz, 1961), pp. 113-14.

[15]"The Current Tasks of the Party's Ideological Work: Report of Secretary of the CPSU Central Committee L. F. Ilyichov at the Plenary Meeting of the CPSU Central Committee, 18 June 1963," *Moscow News, Free Supplement,* No. 25 (652), 22 June 1963, pp. 8, 13.

[16]Cf. 2 Cor. 5:17: "If any one is in Christ, he is a new creation; the old has passed away, behold, the new has come."

[17]See above, chapter 3, note 6.

[18]"He who would not prefer to build the whole world out of his own resources, to be a creator of the world, rather than to be eternally bothering about himself, has already been anathematised by the spirit, he is under an interdict, but in the opposite sense; he is expelled from the temple and deprived of the eternal enjoyment of the spirit and left to sing lullabies about his own private bliss and to dream about himself at night" (from the notebooks on Epicurean philosophy, written before 1841, *Collected Works,* I, 468-69).

[19]From "Thus Spake Zarathustra," trans. Th. Common, *The Complete Works of Friedrich Nietzsche,* ed. Oscar Levy, vol. 11 (New York: Russell and Russell, 1964), p. 255.

[20]Title of the book by Solzhenitsyn's colleague, L. A. Kopelev, trans. and ed. A. Austin (Philadelphia: Lippincott, 1977).

[21]M. Mihajlov, *Mystical Experiences of the Labor Camps,* trans. A. A. Kiselev, Kontinent 2 (Garden City. N.Y.: Anchor Books, Doubleday, 1977), pp. 110-11, 107.

[22]Ibid., pp. 110ff.

[23]Cf. John Calvin, *Institutes of the Christian Religion,* III, chaps. 9, 10.

Chapter Nine: The Genesis of the New Man in Marxism

[1]Cf. P. Spoerri, *Gesucht—der neue Mensch* (In Search for the New Man, my translation), Theologie und Dienst, No. 7, (Giessen and Basel: Brunnen 1975), p. 6-7.

[2]Leonid Ilyichov, p. 16: "A school teacher . . . is . . . the Party's closest ally in educating the new man" (quoting N. Khrushchev).

[3]*Himmat* weekly, Bombay, 24 Sept. 1965.

[4]Hinz, pp. 20ff.

[5]As quoted in Hinz, p. 46.

[6]As quoted in Galina Berkenkopf, *"Neuer Mensch" vor alten Fragen. Sowjetische Schriftsteller und die Herausforderung der Wahrheit* ("New Man" Facing Old Questions. Soviet Writers and the Challenge of Truth) (Berlin, 1972), p. 27.

[7]Hinz, p. 47.

[8]As quoted in Hinz, p. 23.

[9]See the memoirs of his daughter Svetlana Allilueva, *Twenty Letters to a Friend*, trans. Priscilla Johnson (New York: Harper & Row, 1967); and her second book *Only One Year*, trans. Paul Chavchavadze (New York: Harper & Row, 1969).

[10]Ibid., p. 22.

[11]Ibid., p. 29.

[12]Ibid., pp. 21, 26.

[13]Galina Nikolajewa, as quoted by Hinz, p. 30.

[14]As summed up by U. Duchrow, "Die Frage nach dem neuen Menschen in theologischer und marxistischer Anthropologie" (The Problem of the New Man in Theological and Marxist Anthropology) in *Marxismusstudien*, vol. 7, ed. H. F. Tödt (Tubingen: J. C. B. Mohr, 1972), p. 45.

[15]As quoted in Berkenkopf, p. 11.

[16]Duchrow, pp. 50, 57.

[17]A. Tschakowski as quoted in Hinz, p. 43.

[18]As quoted by Berkenkopf, p. 28.

[19]Cf. L. Schapiro, *The Communist Party of the Soviet Union*, p. 203-04.

[20]*Venceremos! The speeches and writings of Ernesto Ché Guevara*, ed. John Gerassi (New York: Macmillan, 1968), p. 391.

[21]Ilyichov, p. 15.

[22]Friedrich Nietzsche, "*Thoughts Out of Season*," trans. A. M. Ludovici, *The Complete Works*, vol. 4, ed. O. Levy (New York: Russell and Russell, 1964).

[23]Josif Ton, "The Christian Manifesto," *Religion in Communist Lands*, Supplementary Paper No. 2, Keston College, England, February 1976.

[24]Cf. Immanuel Kant: "But if *a man* is to *become* not merely *legally*, but *morally*, a good man . . . and one who, knowing something to be his duty, requires no incentive other than this representation of duty itself, *this* cannot be brought about through gradual *reformation* . . . but must be effected through a *revolution* in the man's disposition. . . . He can become a new man only by a kind of rebirth, as it were a new creation (John III, 5; compare also Genesis I, 2) and a change of heart" (from his *Religion within the Limits of Reason Alone*, trans. Th. M. Greene and H. H. Hudson [New York: Harper Torchbooks, 1960], pp. 42-43).

[25]K. Mehnert, *The Anatomy of Soviet Man*, trans. M. Rosenbaum (London: Weidenfeld and Nicholson, 1961), pp. 67ff. This particular statement is only in the enlarged German version, *Der Sowjetmensch* (Frankfurt and Hamburg: Fischer-Bücherei, [No. 388] 1961), p. 361.

[26]As quoted in Spoerri, p. 9.

Chapter Ten: The Christian Response

[1]M. Claudius, *Sämtliche Werke* (Collected Works), pt. 6 (Zurich: Ex Libris, n.d.), p. 420 (my translation). Claudius continues: "One does not turn the hand in order that the works in the clock may go rightly. Similarly, also with man I want to see not only a change of hands, but the improvement of the inner person, so that on the clockface all will be made well by itself."

[2]Article IV (Justification) of Melanchthon's Apology of the Augsburg Confession, in *The Book of Concord: The Confessions of the Evangelical Lutheran Church*, trans. and ed. Th. G. Tappert et al. (Philadelphia: Fortress, 1959), see pp. 131, 143.

[3]*Die Welt*, 18 Nov. 1974.

[4]K. Jaspers, *The Future of Mankind*, trans. E. B. Ashton (Chicago: Univ. of Chicago Press, 1961), pp. 258-60.

Index